Sri Lankan Flavours

A journey through the island's food and culture

Sri Lankan Flavours

A journey through the island's food and culture

Channa Dassanayaka

With Natalee Ward
Photography by Craig Wood

Hardie Grant Books

First published in 2003 by
Hardie Grant Books
85 High Street
Prahran, Victoria 3181, Australia
www.hardiegrant.com.au

National Library of Australia Cataloguing-in-Publication Data:

Dassanayaka, Channa.
Sri Lankan Flavours : a journey through the island's food and culture.

Includes index.
ISBN 174066 066 8

1. Cookery, Sri Lankan. 2. Sri lanka – Description and travel. I. Title.

641.595493

Photography by Craig Wood
Cover design by Pfisterer + Freeman
Internal design and layout by Natalee Ward
Printed and bound in China by SNP Leefung

10 9 8 7 6 5 4 3 2

To my father, mother and grandmother for giving me
the confidence to be me.

Thanks

This book has been as much a journey as the trip to Sri Lanka itself, and there are many people who have helped us rise to the occasion.

In Sri Lanka, we couldn't have done without the help of Ajith and Nishantha, my aunt and uncle, Premasingha and Jayanthi and all my family members. Thanks also to Gerard Menids and Rohan Fernandopulle at Colombo Hilton, and the staff at Kandalama Hotel, in particular Amal Nanayakara and Senaka Perera.

I owe all I have learnt to the principle of the Ceylon Hotel School, Sarath Senavirathna, and to my lecturers in cookery, front office, restaurant, housekeeping and other faculty members.

From Melbourne, a huge thanks to Indika Galhenage at Sigiri in Northcote and Rothitha Ekanayaka, Loku Amma (Prema), Ajantha Ellepola, Maxwell Kegall, and Craig and Rickie Langley. Thanks also to my brothers Sampath and Prassanna Dassanayaka. Thanks to Dur-é Dara for her enduring support and John Mackay, Enza Casiso and Helen Saniga.

Special thanks to Craig for his vision through the lense in what was once a foreign country to him and for his sense of humour on the road. And thanks also to Natalee for her wonderful way with words and layouts.

Eternal thanks to my grandmother. Although she didn't live to see the final product, I know she would have enjoyed this book.

From Craig: Thanks to Manique DeSilva and her parents Ray and Dashnee Parnavitana for the use of their house in Colombo and to Vasantha for her fabulous cooking during our stay. Thanks to Ajith Indrasiri for transporting us around Sri Lanka safely and for being a cool guy. Thanks to Channa's family, in particular his grandmother, uncle and aunt for their amazingly warm hospitality, Shamini Jayamanna for the use of their house in the village, and Asitha Abeywickrama for driving me around the village on his motorbike, spending his time interpreting for me and helping me take great shots. I would also like to thank all the villagers for their assistance.

In Melbourne, thanks to Andrew Tauber for lending me his medium format camera. Good on you, Taubs! Thanks to Supply and Demand, Matchbox and Country Road for their assistance with products and thanks to Andrew Roach, David Cohen and Pauli Aborti for her styling.

Thanks to Nat for taking the project and driving it. Her enthusiasm and energy has been amazing not to mention her considerable talents. And thanks to Channa for a wonderful journey that started over a bowl of tom yum.

From Natalee: Thanks to Channa for taking the time to explain the intricacies of gambodge when it would have been easier to give up, and for his prevailing sense of humour. Thanks also to Craig for his steady supply of stunning images and his constant encouragement. When it came to putting the vision and the words together we couldn't have done without Tracy O'Shaughnessy for her direction and Clare Coney for her attention to detail. Thanks to Hardie Grant for believing in us.

Thanks to Paul Sellars, Brock Lever at Rojay, Pauli Aborti and Murray Johnson for his courier services, advice and general abilities as a tower of strength.

Foreword

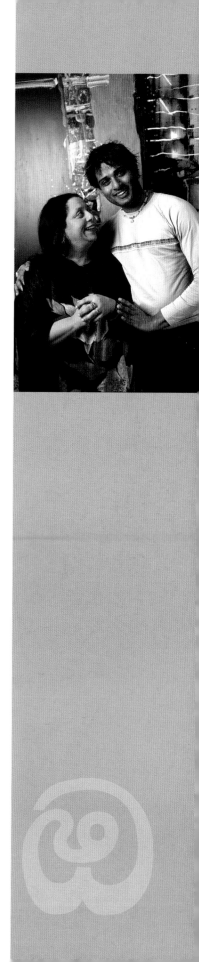

Rather than write a foreword to this book I see it as more appropriate to write a blessing, to speak on behalf of the book simply because I feel good about it.

This book is a personal offering, a collaboration of three people about one person's life and culinary traditions. I am a great believer in people's personal stories and this unique documentation of a life through food, especially if the person is a cook.

Channa Dassanayaka found himself orphaned and in Australia on a work permit without his family, friends or cultural connections. In order to work in Australia, Channa is required to have a guardian. By a chance encounter I became his sponsor, and it has been a pleasure to work with him on his projects and working life.

Today, the Australian palette is so diverse most Australians are well acquainted with Thai, Malaysian, Indian and Chinese food. There is room for acquiring a taste for Sri Lankan food. For this we must acknowledge the work of Charmaine Solomon – she first introduced Sri Lankan food to Australia and remains the leader in the appreciation of this cuisine.

This book is not a definitive guide to Sri Lankan food, but a story of one individual culinary life. As a cookbook it is evocative and enticing to the eater, and it encourages you to explore the cuisine. It will allow you to be more discerning in a Sri Lankan restaurant, and inspire you to cook, to understand the basics of the dish, and to adjust the flavours to suit your palette or culinary desire.

This venture is a shining example of the positive relationships that result from a young cook like Channa coming to Australia. In what is a disturbing time for immigrants in Australia, this is a positive venture, a fine example of how valuable this experience has been for Channa and his new Australian friends.

This document is also a beautiful way in which Channa can make sense of his own story. It is a means by which he can pay tribute to his history, to his mother and grandmother and the family heritage he carries with him. It is also his offering to his life in Australia.

My only contribution to the book has been my encouragement and belief in the project. I wish to congratulate Channa and his co-producers, Craig and Nat, not just in demonstrating a coming together of skills, but for a collaboration that exhibits a shared commitment of talents and friendship and a celebration of diversity.

As Channa's official guardian, I had no real picture of his life or his rich cultural heritage. This book has changed all that and it has been a joy to watch it come to fruition. Channa has also connected me with the home country of my maternal grandparents and my mother and I look forward to returning there one day.

I wish Channa and his collaborators the privilege of having this book received in the way that they have intended.

And most of all bravo,

With my admiration, love and encouragement

Dur-e Dara, Melbourne restaurateur, business woman, musician

Contents

Introduction

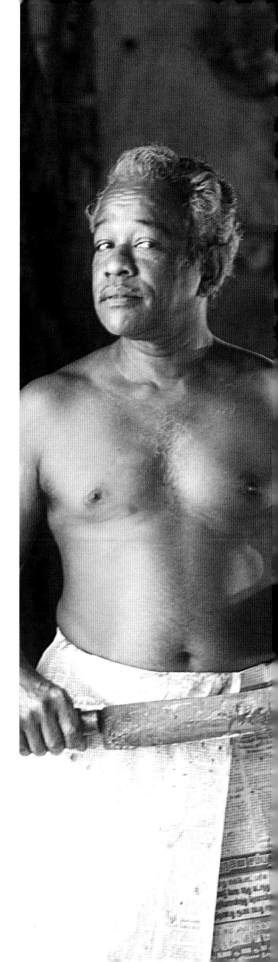

In Ehliyagoda, a small village in Sri Lanka's central hills region, two girls stand above a mortar and pestle, grinding rice into flour with every blow of their large coconut-wood rods. It is heavy work for the young girls.

But preparing food is as much a social occasion as it is a domestic duty in Sri Lanka – a time for women to gather and gossip. Grinding rice is a daily routine that takes place in villages across the country and while the nation's business capital, Colombo, is a modern urban metropolis, beyond the city limits most Sri Lankans live a traditional way of life.

A large portion of the 20 million residents in this tear-shaped country the size of Tasmania are involved in the food industry – as farm hands, selling produce at markets and on the side of the road, or working in restaurants or tea houses, feeding others. You see the evidence of this everywhere … roadside stalls sell fresh meat and fish, red rice and curries or buffalo curd in clay pots. When you buy a King Coconut, a national delicacy, the seller will hack a section off with a machete, place a straw in the top and send you on your way. Boys push trolleys or ride bikes with carts attached selling vegetables and fruit such as bananas, jackfruit, local cherries, cashew nuts and diced mangoes.

Slowly recovering from the ravages of civil war – a ceasefire in December 2001 brought the battles to a halt, and calm now prevails – the nation once known as Ceylon is rebuilding, led by the clothing and gem industries, as well as tea, coconut products and spice exports. And the tourists are beginning to return, although a strong military presence reminds travellers that the country has battled Indian, Portuguese, Dutch and English occupation as well as internal rifts over the past two centuries. But the hotels are filling again as sightseers from across the globe trickle back to this part of Asia.

While international influences can be seen throughout the land, the villages of rural Sri Lanka have retained their traditional way of life. In kitchens across the land, old recipes and food customs are as strong as ever.

The Sri Lankan cuisine is dominated by curries, and while many dishes are similar to those created in neighbouring Asian nations, such as India and Thailand, Sri Lanka's distinctive use of spices, herbs, fresh vegetables and fruit make its cuisine unique.

I was born in Colombo in 1969, and although I grew up in the busy metropolis, much of my time was spent in my grandmother's house in Ehliyagoda, near Ratnapura in the centre of Sri Lanka. My father used to say it was named as 'the village of the women with the beautiful eyes', and it has retained much of Sri Lanka's traditional way of life.

My grandfather was the Gammuladani – the village head, a role similar to a town mayor. Because of this, my mother was educated at a convent and trained in Western etiquette. But she kept her love of Sri Lankan food. She always cooked for the family, no matter how many appeared at the dinner table each night. I was exposed to my mother's cooking from the early days and developed a palate for good food, but it wasn't until I started visiting my grandmother's house and understood her cooking talents that I realised where my mother had learnt her skills. My grandmother's food was soul food, the original food, and my mother used to crave her cooking; I developed these cravings too.

I went to primary school and secondary school in Colombo, but my final year exams were a disaster. Determined to make a lawyer of me, my mother hired a private tutor to take me through my final exams again. However, one day, while I was being tutored in commerce, my mother discovered I was instead sketching food and describing dishes in my notebook.

'I have decided not to send you back to school to study,' she said. 'Instead I will send you to a hotel school.' The profession was frowned upon by my family, who believed I was going to wash dirty dishes for the rest of my life. But I didn't care.

At the Ceylon Hotel School, one of the toughest schools of its kind in the country, I studied restaurant and bar work. After six months I passed well and was sent to Oman in the Middle East to look after the Royal Navy base dining room for the high officers. There I was taught the details of fine dining and I was accepted into the pastry kitchen to help.

One night I encouraged them to host a Sri Lankan feast and from that day, after preparing a wonderful banquet, I was hooked. I returned to the hotel school and once more studied cookery. We learnt about Sri Lankan and international cuisine and studied French and German languages – French culinary terms are essential in cooking. We also studied other restaurant-related subjects, such as food costing and menu planning.

I had a flair for pastry work and after finishing at the school I flew to Germany to practise this talent in a castle in the Black Forest. There we turned the fine dining restaurant into a Sri Lankan restaurant and it was a hit with locals. I ran the kitchen, worked at front of house and learnt to create Sri Lankan cuisine without many of the authentic ingredients, which proved great training.

Working in and studying all the different areas of the restaurant and hotel industry taught me an important lesson – everyone contributes and you have to respect others working in the kitchen. I believe it is important not to become an aggressive chef – some chefs think they are the only people working with hot ovens and knives, but preparing and serving food is a team effort.

I then studied intermediate cookery and later advanced cookery, learning everything from butchery to food handling and nutrition. Over the years spent studying I worked in the Meridian Hotel in Colombo as a commis, making Sri Lankan desserts and pastry. The hotel later became the Marriott and I continued my work there. In my final year of study I was offered a job at the Colombo Hilton under Gerard Mendis, the executive pastry chef.

But civil unrest was always close at hand in Sri Lanka and one day a bomb exploded at the Central Bank next door to the Hilton. There were many civilian casualties. I was very scared – I tried to call home but the phone lines had been cut. Buildings were collapsing around us and I didn't think I was going to survive. The next few days were spent cooking for the emergency crews as they recovered the bodies.

This was not the first time I had been close to the warfare and my family decided I would be better off in another country. In 1996 I packed my bags and moved to

The Dassanayaka family in 1976. Channa is on the far left.

Australia. My mother thought it was a good country, one in which I could reach my potential, and she helped me set up a restaurant in Chapel St, in Melbourne's inner eastern suburb of Prahran. Woodapple became known as one of the best Sri Lankan restaurants in the city.

When my mother died in a car accident in 1997 I returned to Sri Lanka. I stayed for a year, living from time to time in a temple, where I meditated and thought about what life was all about. But I had unfinished business, and I came back to Australia in 1998.

Looking for a fresh start, I helped Indika Galhenage open his restaurant Sigiri in Northcote, working with him on his menu. It is now one of the best Sri Lankan restaurants in Melbourne. Here I met Melbourne restaurateur Dur-é Dara and we clicked instantly. I began working at her restaurant, Lip, in St Kilda under chef Diane Kerry and later joined the team at her Bourke St restaurant Nudle Bar.

Under Dur-é's supervision, chef John Mackay, Enza Casiso and I opened Nudle Bar Two at Southgate. This is where I met Craig, a photographer from the Herald Sun newspaper. He used to eat vegetarian tom yum at the Nudle Bar every day, to the point where we used to call him 'tom yum'. The kitchen there was open and people would sit at the food bar and chat to us as we cooked. Craig and I became friends and started to talk about writing a book on Sri Lankan cuisine.

We planned our trip and were joined by John and Enza. Together the four of us returned to my home country to savour the people, the places, the images and the food of Sri Lanka.

Standards

In general, most of the recipes in this book serve four to six people.

When we eat dinner in Sri Lanka, we don't just serve one curry: there will be several, including a meat or fish curry and one or two vegetarian dishes. One dish on the table will often have a runny consistency while another will be dry. Rice and bread will also be served, as will two or three sambols or chutneys.

Don't stress about curry

Curries are the most common dish in the world, eaten throughout Asia, Europe, Africa, North America and Australia. But when it comes to cooking curries at home, many people think 'curry' and they automatically start to become stressed ... they believe curries are too spicy, or they are just for winter, or they are difficult to make or they just don't understand the ingredients.

It is important not to get stressed when it comes to making curries. Once you become accustomed to cooking them you will discover that the processes involved in cooking all curries, whether they be meat, chicken, fish or vegetable, are generally the same – it is just a matter of changing the main ingredients as you go.

And if you can't find ingredients such as pandanus leaves, curry leaves or Maldive fish – don't stress, simply run without them.

Essential things for a perfect curry

The colour

'White' curries have a bright yellow appearance, while meat curries should look dark red to brown, regardless of how spicy they are. If you prefer a mild curry, use sweet paprika to maintain a bright colour and use turmeric for a beautiful golden orange curry.

The texture

Vegetable curries should be runnier than meat curries. You can make a sauce thicker by lightly roasting two tablespoons each of rice and coconut in a pan and grinding it into a paste. Add a tablespoon of the paste to thicken the curry.

The flavour

As for flavour, curries should have either a chilli kick, a peppery kick or a sour flavour and this comes from the balance of spices. Adjust the chilli flavour to suit your taste and substitute green chillies for red if you want a milder curry. Follow the recipe, but then follow your tastebuds too, sampling the dish as you go in order to get the seasoning balance right.

Curry powder – the key

The key to these dishes is the curry powder. Recipes have been given for curry powder and roasted curry powder (see pages 73-75). You can make a curry blend and keep in an airtight container in the fridge or a dry cupboard for up to a year. Meat curries and fish curries generally use the roasted curry powder, while standard, unroasted curry powder is used in vegetarian curries. However, this rule can be broken.

Varying a curry

For adding extra flavour you can:

- add chicken stock
- add Maldive fish flakes to vegetable curries if you are not concerned about vegetarian issues
- add a cup of diced tomatoes
- finish a curry with a handful of chopped coriander leaves – you can never go wrong with this.

Cooking notes

Sambols

Just as curries can be varied to suit your taste, sambols are also flexible. Each and every sambol is made slightly differently by every cook, depending on whether they prefer chilli, salt or the sour taste of lime or lemon. Always adjust to taste so your preferred balance of flavours comes through.

Tomatoes

I find tomatoes give varying degrees of flavour to a dish. If you need extra acidity to balance coconut milk and the tomatoes just don't have it, add a tablespoon of tomato paste. You can also add a teaspoon of lemon or lime juice to round out the flavours, but only after you have taken the finished dish off the heat.

Ingredients

Most of the ingredients in this book are available in supermarkets but some are only available from specialty Asian and Indian grocery stores or large produce markets. If you are having trouble finding specific ingredients, ask your nearest Indian restaurant for the name of a supermarket which sells these products.

Spices in recipes

Leave them in! Cardamom pods, curry leaves, bay leaves, lemongrass, cloves, cinnamon sticks, pandanus – Sri Lankans serve dishes with all of these presented in the bowl, as it is a sure sign of the authenticity of flavour. The spices are not eaten but simply left on the plate. You can remove them just before serving if you choose.

Coconut milk

If you don't have coconut milk you can finish off a curry by adding normal milk or yoghurt.

Eggs

When I refer to eggs in recipes I mean a 60 g (2 oz) egg.

Oil in recipes

The oil specified in these recipes is olive or vegetable oil, but you can use coconut oil for extra flavour.

Glossary

banana chillies – *malu miris*

Larger than a green chilli but smaller than a capsicum, banana chillies (Hungarian wax chillies) are a milder, sweeter version of the green chilli. Sri Lankans use them in curries or stuff them as a savoury snack.

basil seeds – *khasa khasa*

Basil seeds are used in desserts and drinks such as faluda. When soaked in water these little black seeds with their lemon basil scent develop a gelatinous coating but maintain a crunchy interior, similar to passionfruit seeds.

cardamom – *enasa*

Cardamom has a pungent flavour and is used in curry powders and desserts as well as in tea. The cardamom pod contains tiny black seeds, which can be extracted from the pod, but in many recipes the entire pod is used and discarded before serving, as a bay leaf would be. The spice is native to India.

chickpea flour

Also known as besan flour, chickpea flour is made from a smaller variety of chickpea and is used in batters for deep frying.

chilli – *miris*

You don't get far in Sri Lankan cuisine without using chilli. Fresh green and red chillies are used in curries, along with dried red chilli flakes, ground chilli or chilli powder. Most Sri Lankan kitchens have a jar of salted chillies (see recipe page 101) on hand for adding extra flavour to curries. These can also be deep-fried and served on the side of a main meal as a condiment.

cloves – *karabu nati*

Cloves are dried, unopened flower buds, which add a spicy flavour to curry powders. They need to be used sparingly as they are strong.

coconut milk – *pol kiri*

When buying canned coconut milk, always choose the unsweetened variety, as opposed to standard coconut milk, which is sweetened for use in desserts. Using coconut milk powder allows you to control the thickness of the milk, by adding more or less water depending on the recipe. Coconut milk powder is always unsweetened. You can make your own coconut milk by grating coconut flesh, mixing it with water in a food processor or blender and passing through a sieve to extract the milk. The flesh of 1 coconut takes about 3 cups of water to produce a thick milk. When you choose a coconut to buy, make sure you shake it to listen for the water inside. This indicates the flesh will be fresh.

coriander – *kothamalli*

Fresh coriander leaves have a strong lemon peel and sage flavour and are chopped and sprinkled over curry dishes. Coriander seeds also have a lemon flavour, and are roasted and ground to form a key component of curry powders. They are best used freshly ground for maximum flavour.

cumin – *suduru*

Pale brown cumin seeds have a strong, earthy flavour with a dried peppermint tinge and are essential to Sri Lankan curry powders. They are similar to fennel seeds but smaller.

curry leaves – *karapincha*

Curry leaves don't taste like curry at all; their name comes from their essential role in curry dishes. The leaves are from the native Sri Lankan curry tree (Murraya koenigii) and have a citrus aroma – the tree belongs to the same family as oranges and lemons. The leaves can be used fresh or dried and are added to the pan with oil when you begin to make a curry. If you can't find curry leaves, use one or two bay leaves instead – it's not an ideal substitute as bay leaves don't give the same flavour, but they will do the job.

curry powders, roasted and unroasted

Unroasted curry powder – or simply, curry powder – is mainly used in vegetarian curries while roasted curry powder has a darker colour and stronger flavour and is frequently used in meat curries. Unroasted curry powder is the standard powder you buy in supermarkets while roasted curry powder is a bit more of a specialty and is found in Asian or Indian supermarkets. You can make your own mix following recipes on pages 73-75.

dhal

Dhal is the collective name for a wide variety of pulses (dried beans and peas) that are eaten daily in Sri Lankan homes in some form or other and that provide a valuable source of protein. Dhal is also the name for the dish itself, which is a thickish purée eaten with rice or bread. It is a popular breakfast dish and an essential component of every meal. See also urad dhal.

dried shrimp – *kunisso*

These tiny dried shrimp have a strong flavour and are used mainly in sambols and mallums. They can be bought from Asian groceries and good supermarkets.

fennel seeds – *maduru*

Fennel seeds are similar in appearance to cumin seeds but have a sweet aniseed flavour. They are used in curry powders.

fenugreek – *uluhaal*

A member of the pea family, fenugreek's flat brown seeds are used dried in curry dishes, particularly vegetable and seafood dishes. Sometimes fennel seeds are soaked in water overnight, when they develop a gelatinous coating which is used as a thickening agent for curries.

ghee – *elengethel*

Ghee, or clarified butter, is popular in Indian and Sri Lankan cooking and can be heated to a higher temperature than butter. It is bought in cans at supermarkets.

gambodge – *goraka*

Gambodge (also known as kokam in many Western cultures) is a fruit similar to an orange and is used as a souring agent, in a similar fashion to tamarind. The fruit is bright orange when ripe, but is used dried in cooking, when the fruit segments have shrivelled to small black leathery pieces. Gambodge is used in fish and pork curries, mostly in pieces so it can be removed before eating.

jaggery – *hakuru or jaggery*

Also known as gulab melaka, jaggery is unrefined sugar from a palm tree or sugar cane and is commonly used in desserts.

lemongrass – *sera*

Lemongrass is another integral part of the curry flavour. Use the white section of the stalk only and bruise it with a mortar and pestle or the side of a knife to release the flavour. Lemongrass is often left whole in the dish and discarded before serving, or served but not eaten.

Maldive fish – *umbalakade*

Maldive fish, also known as dried tuna, is actually dried bonito fish, caught in the South China Sea and processed on the Maldive Islands which neighbour Sri Lanka. Few Sri Lankan dishes are served without Maldive fish flakes – some dishes are enhanced with a mere sprinkling of the dried fish while others, such as sambols, are carried by the flavour.

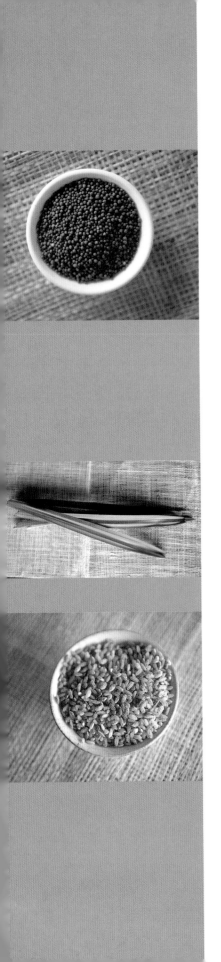

mustard seeds – *aba*

Brown mustard seeds can be bought in supermarkets and are used whole or ground in curries. If used whole, sauté in oil with curry leaves and onion until they 'pop' and release their flavours – about 30 seconds.

okra – *bandakka*

Okra are also known as lady's fingers or gumbo. These green ribbed seed pods offer a good supply of vitamins A and C, as well as fibre, calcium and iron and are often used in Sri Lankan vegetable curries and dry stir-fries with Maldive fish.

pandanus – *rampe*

The stiff, bright green pandan leaf is used for its colour and flavour in curries and rice dishes. There is no substitute for the unusual nutty, grassy flavour of the leaf, which is cut into pieces and added to a dish, but removed prior to eating, or served as a garnish but not eaten.

red rice

Unpolished or unrefined rice, which contains more fibre than polished rice. Like brown rice, it takes longer to cook than white rice and can be bought from organic shops, Asian groceries and good supermarkets.

rose syrup

A sweet rose syrup that can be bought from Asian grocery stores or made from equal quantities of fragrant rose petals, sugar and water, boiled for 10–15 minutes or until the mixture forms a thick syrup.

snake beans – *ma-karal*

Snake beans are also known as asparagus bean, yard-long bean and Chinese long bean. The long, dark green beans are popular in Sri Lanka as a curry dish.

sweet paprika

This bright red powdered spice is used for colour as an alternative to chilli powder – perfect for those who prefer a milder dish without losing any of the spicy look.

tamarind – *siyambala*

The pulp of tamarind pods adds a sour flavour to dishes, usually fish and meat curries. You can buy tamarind as a pod, dried in a block, or as a concentrate in jars from Asian grocery stores.

turmeric powder – *kaha*

This bright orange rhizome, which looks like a small version of ginger, is used in Sri Lankan cuisine for its vibrant yellow colour. Water coloured with turmeric is sprinkled in Sri Lankan houses for good luck. It is a good substitute for the more expensive spice saffron.

urad dhal

This comes in two forms. It is white in colour when hulled and split, or black when the grains are unhulled and whole. Urad dhal is also known as black gram. Use green or yellow split peas as an alternative.

water spinach – *kangkung*

Water spinach leaves are long, pointed dark green leaves which, like spinach, require very little cooking. They are ideal for stir-fries and are a common green vegetable in Sri Lankan cuisine.

Conversion tables

Volume

Metric	Imperial
50–55 ml	2 fl oz
75 ml	3 fl oz
100 ml	3½ fl oz
120 ml	4 fl oz
150 ml	5 fl oz
170 ml	6 fl oz
200 ml	7 fl oz
225 ml	8 fl oz
300 ml	10 fl oz
400 ml	13 fl oz
500 ml	17 fl oz
600 ml	20 fl oz
750 ml	25 fl oz
1 litre	34 fl oz

Note:

A pint in the US contains 16 fl oz; a pint in the UK contains 20 fl oz.

Teaspoons, tablespoons and cups

This book uses metric cup measurements, i.e. 250 ml for 1 cup. In the US a cup is 8 fl oz, just smaller, and American cooks should be generous in their cup measurements. In the UK a cup is 10 fl oz and British cooks should be scant with their cup measurements.

1 teaspoon	5 ml
1 tablespoon	15 ml
1 cup	250 ml

Weight

Metric	Imperial
10–15 g	½ oz
20 g	¾ oz
30 g	1 oz
40 g	1½ oz
50–60 g	2 oz
75 g	2½ oz
80 g	3 oz
100 g	3½ oz
125 g	4 oz
150 g	5 oz
175 g	6 oz
200 g	7 oz
225 g	8 oz
250 g	9 oz
275 g	10 oz
300 g	10½ oz
350 g	12 oz
400 g	14 oz
450 g	1 lb
500 g	1 lb 2 oz
650 g	1½ lb
900 g	2 lb
1 kg	2 lb 3 oz

Temperature

°C	°F
140	275
150	300
160	320
170	340
180	350
190	375
200	400
210	410
220	430

Length

Metric	Imperial
5 mm	¼ in
1 cm	½ in
2 cm	¾ in
2.5 cm	1 in
5 cm	2 in
7.5 cm	3 in
10 cm	4 in
15 cm	6 in
20 cm	8 in
30 cm	12 in

the daily grind

rice and breads

Whether one eats at a roadside stall or inside the home, rice and breads form the base of all Sri Lankan cuisine.

The rice served is typically a medium- to short-grained, non-aromatic variety, and comes in three guises.

• The type of rice served most frequently is red rice, so called because it is unpolished or unrefined. Its extra nutritional value lies in the fact that it contains more fibre than polished rice, akin to eating rye instead of white bread. It is served steamed at most meals.

• Milk rice, kiribath, is served at any Sri Lankan festival, religious or otherwise, and on special occasions such as birthdays.

• Saffron rice is Sri Lanka's night-time festival dish. Being such an expensive spice, saffron is, in fact, not commonly cooked with rice, other than among the wealthy. Instead, to produce the desired colour, turmeric is generally used instead.

And with every curry and rice meal an accompanying bread is also prepared. Roti is served plain on the table and dipped into a dhal or curry, or made into a small parcel filled with a spicy curry as a delicious snack.

Hoppers – small, bowl-shaped pancakes made from rice flour and coconut milk – are one of the most distinctive elements of a Sri Lankan meal. With an egg cooked in the middle, hoppers can be eaten alone or mixed with curries and other dishes. Stringhoppers, little circles of tangled noodles made from rice flour and water, are also popular, dipped in curries and sambols and enjoyed for breakfast, lunch or dinner.

Yellow rice

This is my mother's version of a popular Sri Lankan dish, which is great to serve if you are out to impress your dinner guests – rich in flavour and colourful on the table. My mother's secret was that she always added chopped coriander and natural yoghurt to the rice just before serving. They give a beautiful aroma, and balance the sweet flavours of the nuts and sultanas.

2 cups basmati rice

3½ cups water, vegetable stock or chicken stock

1 teaspoon ground turmeric

1 teaspoon salt

2 cloves

3 cardamom pods, crushed

6 curry leaves (or 1 bay leaf)

1 cinnamon stick

6 peppercorns

2 tablespoons ghee or butter

50 g (2 oz) raw cashews

50 g (2 oz) sultanas

½ cup chopped coriander (cilantro) leaves (optional)

2 tablespoons natural yoghurt (optional)

Rinse rice thoroughly with water until the water runs clear – about 2–3 minutes.

Put water or stock in a pot over medium heat, add turmeric, salt, cloves, cardamom, curry leaves, cinnamon and peppercorns and bring to boil. Stir briefly and add the rice. Cover with a tight-fitting lid and simmer for 20–25 minutes then remove from the heat.

In a little pan on medium heat, melt the ghee or butter, add cashews and sultanas and sauté until golden brown. Add the mixture to the rice and mix well.

Either serve as is or stir through coriander and yoghurt just before serving.

Serves 4–6.

Tip

Ghee is used in Indian cooking and, although it has a high fat content, it gives a wonderful flavour.

Kiribath
coconut rice

Kiribath, or coconut rice, is a popular dish with cultural significance. The dish is traditionally the first solid food given to a baby and it is also very often served at weddings.

250 g (9 oz) red rice or white rice

75 g (2½ oz) coconut milk
  powder

750 ml (25 fl oz) water

1 tablespoon salt

4 cardamom pods, crushed and
  seed cases removed

10 g (½ oz) butter, melted

Wash and drain rice and set aside. Mix coconut milk powder with water to make a coconut milk.

Place rice in a pot with 500 ml (17 fl oz) of the coconut milk. Add salt and cardamom and simmer over low heat for 30 minutes.

When liquid has evaporated, add the remaining coconut milk. Stir well and cook until the liquid has absorbed and the rice is thick and sticky. Spread milk rice on a greased and lined tray and smooth over with a piece of grease-proof paper or a knife dipped in the melted butter.

It can be served hot or cold. If hot, serve in a bowl. If cold, cut into diamond-shaped pieces when set and serve on a large platter or banana leaf.

Kiribath accompanies chicken or fish curry, lunu miris or seeni sambol, or any dish that doesn't have coconut milk in it.

Serves 4–6.

Lazy rice
Sri Lankan fried rice

This dish was always a quick fix for my mother, who would use food remaining in the fridge to keep the household satisfied before the main meal arrived.

You can make it whenever you are hungry, using whatever you have in the house - a few carrots left in the kitchen, cooked meat or a can of tuna - as long as you have some left-over cooked rice.

1–2 eggs

1 teaspoon sesame oil

pinch of salt

pinch of sugar

1 teaspoon oil

¼ cup chopped onion

50 g (2 oz) bacon, thinly sliced or ¼ cup sausage, ham, salami, chicken, mince (ground beef), canned tuna or whatever meat you have in the fridge. Any two can be used

1 cup cooked rice

½ cup julienned carrot

2 tablespoons green peas

¼ teaspoon freshly ground black pepper

salt to taste

½ cup bean shoots

extra 1 tablespoon sesame oil

shallots or spring onions (optional)

Beat the eggs – one or two, depending on how much egg you like in the dish – with a little sesame oil, a sprinkle of water and a pinch of salt and sugar.

Heat oil in a pan over medium heat and pour in egg mixture to cover base of pan like a thin pancake. As soon as the bottom is sealed, tilt the pan up and, using a spatula, roll the egg pancake up like a carpet would be rolled up. Remove from the pan, place on a chopping board and slice into pieces crossways, about 1 cm (½ in) thick.

Heat a wok on high heat, add 1 teaspoon oil and cover wok with oil. Add onions and cook about 30 seconds. If you are using raw meat, add to wok and seal, breaking continuously with a spoon until cooked through. Add any bacon, cooked meat or tuna to wok and stir, tossing frequently. Add rice and carrots, cook for a few minutes then add peas, pepper and salt to taste and toss thoroughly. Add bean shoots, stir through with a sprinkle of sesame oil and remove from heat.

Serve rice with egg mixed through. If desired, chop a handful of shallots or spring onions and sprinkle over.

Serves 1 or 2.

Steamed rice

You can use white or brown rice for this recipe, but remember that brown rice takes a little longer to cook.

2 cups long-grain or
   medium-grain rice

4 cups water

½ teaspoon salt

5 curry leaves (or 1 bay leaf)

2 cardamom pods

2 cloves

1 cinnamon stick

1 teaspoon vegetable oil

Rinse rice in cold water in a strainer or wash in a bowl until water runs clear – about 2–3 minutes. Drain rice in a strainer.

Place water in a big pot over high heat and bring it to the boil. Add rice and salt, spices and oil and stir through. Lower heat and cover with a fitted lid. Simmer for 30–35 minutes (40 minutes for brown rice) without removing lid, until water is totally absorbed. Remove from heat but keep the lid on for another 5 minutes.

Remove the lid, fluff rice with a fork and remove cardamom pods before serving.

Serves 4.

Tip

It is important not to let the steam escape when cooking rice, so if you have to check the rice, do so quickly. In Sri Lanka we place a brick on the lid of the pot to stop any steam escaping.

This is a common sight in Sri Lanka – a roadside shop spruiking all the available dishes of the day. On the menu is rice and curry, bread with vegetables, hoppers and egg hoppers, short eats, cool drinks, ice cream, yoghurt and wattalappan – a form of egg custard with palm sugar and cashews.

These roadside shops usually don't mark the prices and it is a good idea to ask about the cost of the food before you order.

Ghee rice or buttered rice

Ghee rice is a festive dish and thus rich in flavour, so we always served it with a light curry.

2 cups basmati or
  medium-grained rice

3 tablespoons ghee or butter

10 cm (4 in) piece of rampe
  (pandanus leaf) (optional)

10 curry leaves (or 2 bay leaves)

½ cup chopped onion

4 cups water or stock (chicken or
  vegetable)

½ teaspoon salt

6 peppercorns

50 g (2 oz) sultanas or raisins

Rinse rice thoroughly with water until the water runs clear – about 2–3 minutes.

Melt the ghee or butter in a pan over medium heat, taking care not to let it burn. Add rampe, curry leaves and onion and sauté for about 30 seconds. Add rice and sauté for about 1 minute, stirring with a wooden spoon, until every piece of rice is covered with butter. Add water or stock, salt and peppercorns and cover with a lid.

Bring to the boil, reduce heat and simmer for 20–25 minutes. Remove from heat; stir in sultanas and serve.

Serves 4.

the daily grind

While Colombo is a modern urban city, much of the traditional Sri Lankan way of life still exists in the villages across the country. One of the essential activities in Sri Lankan cooking is grinding ingredients with a mortar and pestle. Hours are spent pounding rice into flour for breads or hoppers, or grinding spices, herbs and chillies for curry powders and sambols.

Every kitchen in Sri Lanka has a mortar and pestle, if not a couple, as well as a grinding stone, which grinds smaller items such as herbs, spices and chillies, and ingredients for sambols, and I used to love the aromas that were embedded in them. However, for pounding rice in a village there would normally be one large mortar and pestle. In my grandmother's village it was kept in her kitchen and rice was stored in huge wooden crates at my grandmother's house.

The daughters of the women and men who worked with my grandparents in the village or in my grandmother's kitchen would meet to pound her rice into flour. While working they would also pound a portion of rice for their own family. My grandmother's mortar and pestle was large – about 1 metre tall and 60 cm wide – and up to four people can work together at such a large mortar, with rhythmic, synchronised pounding.

Working the mortar and pestle is more than just a job of labour; it is the time women come together and talk about the day's news. The girls whose job it is to pound the rice are usually about 17 to 20 years of age, but if older women are working at the mortar and pestle they tend to work in their own group – you pound with your peers. I would listen as the young girls talked about what had happened at school, while women talked about who was going to the temple or village activities, the price of things at the market or whether the rain was going to make it difficult to work at the rubber plantation.

My grandmother's kitchen was made out of cow dung, so you couldn't pound in the kitchen. But together, two people could move the mortar outside.

As a little child I used to sit on the giant mortar. It had a small lid on it, and each morning I would sit there and drink my cup of tea or coffee. My grandmother made fantastic coffee. We had a strand of coffee trees in the backyard and my grandmother used to grind the coffee beans and brew a strong shot of coffee. She would add the coffee to steaming hot milk. I was always given the choice to drink it with jaggery – palm sugar – or regular sugar.

Women working in the kitchen used to drink the tea and have sugar on their palm, which they would lick as they drank. I loved to copy them, but whenever I did, I used to get in trouble with my grandmother.

She always made me feel welcome in the kitchen, even though most people didn't like a young boy staying with women, cooking and acting as they did. Most people want their sons to be doctors and engineers.

'What are you going to be when you grow up – a doctor, a lawyer or an engineer?' I would be asked, and would think: 'Here we go again – I don't want to be any of those. I want to cook.'

Biriyani

This is the queen of rice dishes, served by people who are going all out to show their wealth. Everyone thinks it is a difficult dish to make, but this recipe is simple.

1 quantity Yellow Rice
(see page 5)

4 eggs, hard-boiled and halved

coriander (cilantro) leaves,
for garnish

Chicken curry

2 tablespoons oil

2 cardamom pods

1 bay leaf

1 medium onion, chopped

2 cloves

1 teaspoon crushed garlic

1 teaspoon crushed ginger

500 g (1 lb 2 oz) chicken
maryland (leg and thigh), skin
and bones removed and cut
into 3 cm (1 in) cubes

½ teaspoon ground turmeric

½ teaspoon Roasted Curry Powder
(see page 74)

½ teaspoon paprika or chilli
powder

1 cup chopped or canned
tomatoes

1 teaspoon ground black pepper

1 teaspoon salt

1 cup yoghurt

½ cup chopped coriander
(cilantro) leaves

Onion mixture

4 tablespoons butter

2 onions, sliced into rings

1 cinnamon stick

10 curry leaves (or 2 bay leaves)

Variations

● You can deep-fry the eggs once you have removed the shell. Deep-fry for 2 minutes then cut the eggs in half. These eggs have a wonderful, festive look.

● You can also add a few drops of rose essence or rose water to the dish before cooking it, if you have any.

Chicken curry

Heat the oil in a heavy-based pan over medium heat. Bruise cardamom with the back of a spoon and add to pan with the bay leaf, onion, cloves, garlic, ginger and chicken. Sauté for 5 minutes until chicken is brown and onions are cooked. Add turmeric, curry powder and paprika or chilli and cook for a further 2 minutes. Add tomatoes and mix thoroughly.

Taste and add pepper and salt as desired and cook until chicken is cooked through – about another 7 minutes.

Remove pan from heat, add yoghurt and coriander (cilantro) leaves and mix thoroughly.

Onion mixture

Heat the butter in a pan over medium heat and sauté onion rings and cinnamon for about 2 minutes, then add the curry leaves and sauté for a further 30 seconds. Set aside.

To assemble

Preheat the oven to 200°C (400°F).

In the base of a baking dish place 2 tablespoons of water and a sprinkle of oil, to stop the rice sticking. Spread one-third of the rice over the base of the dish, then layer half the curry on top of the rice. Spread another third of the rice across the curry. Sprinkle half the onion and butter mixture over the rice. Cover with the remaining curry and then with a final layer of rice.

Make a few holes in the layers with the handle of a spoon to allow the steam to escape from the bottom. Cover dish with a lid or aluminium foil and bake in oven for 20 minutes.

Remove from the oven and serve on a dish, garnished with the rest of the onion mixture, halved eggs and coriander (cilantro) leaves.

Serves 4–6.

Stringhoppers

Despite the fact that they share a name, stringhoppers are nothing like the bowl-shaped hoppers. Stringhoppers are little mats of rice vermicelli eaten with curry sauces, chutney and sambols. The method takes time to learn and longer to master, but once you have it you will be rewarded with every meal.

500 g (1 lb 2 oz) Chinese rice flour (available in Asian grocery stores) or standard rice flour

1½ teaspoons salt

750 ml (25 fl oz) water

Prepare a steamer on a pot of boiling water.

Put flour and salt in a bowl and mix thoroughly with a spoon. Make a well in the middle. Add water, stirring continuously. Don't over mix – dough should be ready to use in 3–4 minutes of mixing at the most. The dough should resemble a pasta dough: it should be strong but not tough.

Fill the stringhopper mould with the dough and squeeze the dough out through the holes in the base, moving the mould in a circular motion, to totally cover a stringhopper mat beneath the mould. The hoppers should be about 10 cm (4 in) in diameter and should take about two rotations of the mould to make. Flick the mould upwards to break the dough threads.

Stack mats on top of each other and place in the steamer. Cover with a lid, return water to the boil and steam for 10–12 minutes. Remove mats from the steamer and, while still hot, take each stringhopper off its mat. Squeeze more dough onto the mats and repeat steaming; continue making batches until dough is used up.

Serve warm with curries and sambols.

Makes about 40, which serves about 6.

While they are simple, you need a little equipment to make stringhopper. The stringhopper moulds and mats are available from Indian grocery stores and are quite inexpensive. Instead of mats, you can squeeze the dough onto cooling racks with closely spaced grids, but there is no alternative for a stringhopper mould, which churns out a shower spray of thin pasta strings.

keeping the beat

In traditional Sri Lankan culture, drums are used in festivals, ceremonies and at religious occasions and many young men take apprenticeships as eastern drummers or enter the world of music by following in their father's footsteps.

Young drummers follow their gurus, or teachers, and must wait until they are given a blessing from the teacher before they can work as a drummer independently. How long it takes to receive the blessing depends on their talent and personality.

life in the paddies

Most of the paddies are worked by people who don't actually own the land. Rather than commute every day from their homes to the paddies, the workers build a temporary hut in the middle of the field they are working in and stay there until the harvest is complete.

They use local building materials such as hay and the trunks and branches of coconut trees.

Hoppers

Hoppers are crispy, bowl-shaped pancakes made with rice flour that are eaten for breakfast, lunch or dinner. They are a traditional hawker street food often sold in little shops on the side of the road or from a cart attached to a bicycle. Neon signs in towns and villages announce fresh hoppers ready to eat.

Hoppers come in different varieties and can be sweet or savoury, while an egg hopper has an egg in the middle added during cooking. Tamils often include coconut milk for extra flavour. Hoppers aren't easy to make and you have to have a hopper pan to create them. Once mastered, however, they are one of the great traditions of Sri Lankan food.

1 large coconut and 750 ml (25 fl oz) water or 750 ml (25 fl oz) coconut milk

1 kg (2 lb 3 oz) red rice flour, Chinese rice flour or plain rice flour

1 teaspoon yeast

3 eggs

4 teaspoons salt

5 teaspoons sugar

Tips

- Red rice flour is available in packets from supermarkets.
- You can also buy instant hopper mix from Asian supermarkets.

If you are making coconut milk from scratch, scrape the coconut using a coconut scraper to remove the flesh and place it in a food processor. Pulse blend until soft. Put the coconut in a bowl, add water and mix well. Extract the coconut milk that results by passing the mixture through a sieve into a container.

Put the flour and yeast in a large bowl. Add eggs and 400 ml (13 fl oz) of the coconut milk to the bowl and mix well. Cover and leave to stand for 45 minutes. Then add remaining coconut milk, salt and sugar and mix well until the mixture reaches a thick batter consistency.

Heat the hopper pan over a high flame, put 80 ml (3 fl oz) of batter in it and swirl the batter round to coat the sides of the pan. Cover the pan with a lid, reduce the heat to low and cook for 2½ minutes.

Remove hopper from the pan with a spatula when the edges are slightly brown. Place hot hoppers in a cane basket lined with a banana leaf and serve with chicken or fish curry. I tear the hoppers in half and use them as tongs for sambols and curries.

Makes 18–20.

Variations

• After you put the hopper batter in the pan and turn it around, break an egg into the pan. Cover the pan with a lid and heat over a low flame until the egg is cooked.

• Use freshly scraped coconut to make the coconut milk rather than using coconut milk powder. This gives the hopper its true coconut flavour and adds an essential strength to the batter.

• To make honey hoppers, add ½ cup honey to half a quantity of batter made by this recipe. In Sri Lanka, these hoppers are eaten as a dessert with bananas.

Pol roti
coconut roti

These versatile breads are served at all meals. The coconut flavour teams well with curries, sambols, pickles and chutney. They are best cooked on a roti pan, but a flat griddle, hot plate, barbecue or non-stick fry pan will suffice.

2 cups plain (all-purpose) flour

1 cup desiccated (shredded) coconut

1 teaspoon butter

1 green chilli, chopped

½ onion, chopped

½ teaspoon salt

1 cup water

Mix all ingredients except the water in a bowl, adding salt to taste. Then add water slowly, mixing steadily, until mixture is stiff but malleable. You may not need all the water. Knead well for 2 minutes.

Divide dough into small balls, slightly larger than a golf ball, and flatten out to 5 mm (¼ in) thick on a lightly greased tray. The disks should be about 10 cm (4 in) diameter. Remove from tray, and cook on a pre-heated roti pan – or on a griddle or in a non-stick pan – on medium-low heat for 2–3 minutes each side, until they are lightly browned.

Makes 5 rotis.

essential
ingredients

sambols, pickles and chutneys

No main meal is served at a Sri Lankan table without sambols, chutneys or pickles: little bowls filled with flavour are scattered on the dinner table to provide an additional dimension of intense and vivid flavour.

These dishes are made from a base of salt, lime, Maldive fish flakes – dried tuna fish flakes – and onion. Spices, chillies, herbs and other ingredients are then freshly ground and added to the base just as the meal is being prepared.

With any given meal, Sri Lankans always create one or two of a dozen different sambols to offset the dishes being served. The sambols might, for example, be caramelised onion and chilli, soothing cucumber and yoghurt, or dried shrimp and coconut. Each sambol has its own unique combination of flavours and the taste of curries can be altered depending on the sambol added.

By eating these delicacies in small portions with their hands or with ripped pieces of bread used as scoops, Sri Lankans ensure the flavours of a sambol or pickle are worked thoroughly into their rice and curries.

Some sambols and most of the pickles and chutneys can be kept in jars for months, ready to be served with breads alongside steaming bowls of rice, curry and vegetables.

Kunisso sambol
dried shrimp and coconut sambol

This dish takes about 30 minutes to make but it is worth the work.

½ cup dried shrimp

3 tablespoons oil

1½ cups desiccated (shredded) coconut

2 onions, thinly sliced

1 tablespoon crushed red chillies

10 curry leaves

1 teaspoon paprika

½ cup Maldive fish flakes

salt, to taste

juice of 1 lime

Cover shrimp with water and soak for 30 minutes. Drain and set aside.

Heat half the oil in a pan over medium heat. Add shrimp and sauté until they become golden brown – about 2 minutes. Take shrimp out of the pan with a slotted spoon and place on absorbent paper to drain.

Using the same pan, add remaining oil and the coconut and brown slightly – about 30 seconds. Add onion, chillies, curry leaves, paprika and Maldive fish and cook for a further minute until golden brown. Add salt to mixture then shrimps. Cook until the mixture is crispy and golden. Remove from heat and finish off with lime juice.

Serve with pieces of bread, which are used to scoop up the sambol.

Serves 6.

Thosai sambol
coconut and tamarind sambol

Anyone who tries this dish loves it. This is a wet sambol, served runny. It can accompany any main meal and I like to add it to cheese and tomato sandwiches.

45 g (1½ oz) tamarind pulp

1 cup warm water

4 green chillies

2 cloves garlic, crushed

1 tablespoon crushed ginger

½ teaspoon ground turmeric

1 teaspoon salt

1 cup desiccated (shredded)
coconut – about 75 g (2½ oz)

Soak tamarind pulp in water for 10 minutes. Strain it, discarding pulp.

Place chillies, garlic and ginger in a food processor and pulse into a paste (some processors won't blend very small amounts: if you have trouble you may have to pound using a mortar and pestle). Add turmeric, salt and coconut. Process. Add tamarind liquid to food processor and mix well.

This sambol keeps in the fridge for a week.

Serves 6.

Mint sambol

This sambol is beautiful served with biryani or lamb curry – you need just a little as the flavour is quite strong.

1 cup fresh mint leaves, tightly packed

1 onion, chopped

4 cloves garlic, sliced

⅔ cup desiccated (shredded) coconut

¼ cup sultanas

1 green chilli, sliced

¼ teaspoon salt

½ teaspoon freshly ground black pepper

juice of ½ a lime

Wash and drain mint leaves. Place in a food processor or mortar and pestle and grind with onion, garlic, coconut, sultanas and chilli. Season with salt, pepper and lime juice.

Serves 6–8.

my grandmother

The greatest single source of inspiration for my cooking has been my grandmother. She died in December 2002 at the age of 98, although no birth certificate was registered when she was born and it is generally believed she had lived for more than a century.

Her home was Ehliyagoda, a little village an hour's drive east of Colombo where my grandfather was the *Gammuladani* – the village head. My grandparents owned much of the village and gave a lot of land to charity. They also employed most of the village people in different areas, from the rice paddies to their kitchen.

The family were well known and owned gem pits, rubber plantations and rice paddies. My grandparents had a car, which most people didn't have at the time, and they also had a horse and a couple of elephants, which were a sign of wealth. When women wished to get a message through to my grandfather – whether it was regarding a family problem, financial issues, or a situation within the village – they always approached the lady of the house, my grandmother.

She was a fantastic lady and the village ran smoothly because of it. She was the custodian of the village's traditions, and my grandmother knew exactly which dish should be served for all manner of occasions and festivals. When my grandfather didn't have time for all his duties, my grandmother stepped in for him, attending weddings and social gatherings. She had a huge set of keys, which she used to put in her *osariya* – the Kandyan form of a sari. The longest key, the one for the front door, would be stuck in the sari, the rest of the little keys – about 15–20 – would hang around her tiny waist. The keys opened all the rooms and the cupboards where she kept everything from the rice and gems to her precious memories.

My grandmother had four sons and four daughters, 31 grandchildren, and about 36 great-grandchildren. There were even a couple of great-great-grandchildren at the time she died.

I was one of my grandmother's favourites. I would stay with her when I was growing up and in my school holidays. She never had to yell at me, as she had to at my brothers who were always diving in the rivers. I was interested in cooking and always listened to her when she explained dishes to the people who worked in the kitchen.

'I need a crunch in this dish,' she would say, or 'I need the flavour to come out in this dish', or 'At this stage in cooking, this flavour needs to come out'.

She has been an eternal source of inspiration through her wisdom, her passion and enthusiasm, her deep understanding of Sri Lanka's customs and of the ingredients, flavours and the cultural significance of its cuisine, which she so lovingly passed on to me.

Pol sambol
coconut sambol

Serve with buttered bread, in a roti, or as a side dish with legume curries. It can also be served with stringhoppers or as a side dish with red rice.

½ cup chopped onion

2 green chillies

1 clove garlic

1 teaspoon dried red chilli flakes

1 teaspoon chilli powder

5 curry leaves

3 teaspoons Maldive fish flakes

1 teaspoon salt

1 teaspoon ground black pepper

1 cup desiccated (shredded) coconut

juice of ½ a lime

Place onion, chilli, garlic, chilli flakes, chilli powder, curry leaves and Maldive fish flakes in a food processor and blend. Add the salt, pepper and coconut and blend until mixture is bound.

Remove from food processor and put in a bowl, mix in lime juice and serve.

Serves 6.

Tip

If you double the quantities, add ⅓ cup warm water to the mixture.

Lunu miris
dried chillies, onion and fish sambol

100 g (3½ oz) dried chillies
25 g (1 oz) Maldive fish flakes
1 onion, chopped
salt
juice of 1 lime

Grind chillies, Maldive fish and onion into a coarse paste using a mortar and pestle or food processor. Add salt and lime juice to taste.

Serve with hoppers, roti or curries. Store in an airtight container.

Serves 6.

Seeni sambol
caramelised onion with dried fish and spices

100 ml (3½ fl oz) vegetable oil

10 curry leaves

3 cardamom pods, bruised

1 cinnamon stick

3 cloves

10 cm (4 in) piece of rampe (pandanus leaf)

5 cm (2 in) piece of lemongrass, white part only, bruised

500 g (1 lb 2 oz) onions, sliced

3 teaspoons chilli powder

50 g (2 oz) Maldive fish flakes, crushed to small pieces using a grinder or food processor

salt

2 teaspoons sugar

80 g (3 oz) tamarind pulp, soaked in warm water for 15 minutes

Heat oil in a pan. Sauté curry leaves, cardamom, cinnamon, cloves, rampe and lemongrass for 5 minutes. Add onions and chilli powder and sauté over low heat for about 10 minutes, or until ingredients have browned. Add Maldive fish, salt and sugar and sauté well. Drain liquid from tamarind, discard pulp and add liquid to pan. Simmer for 2 minutes. Remove lemongrass before serving.

Serves 10–12.

Tomato and onion sambol

This is a lovely dish, great for any meat or vegetable curries accompanied with rice and also well suited to Western beef dishes. Or serve in a sandwich or a roti wrap with chicken.

4 large tomatoes

juice of 1 lime or lemon

1 teaspoon chopped green chilli

¾ teaspoon salt

1 large red onion, thinly sliced

½ teaspoon Maldive fish flakes
   (optional)

Cut tomatoes in half, then slice thinly. Set aside.

Soak all ingredients except tomatoes in lime juice for half an hour. This takes the raw flavour out of the onion and gives the dish a pickled flavour.

When it is time to serve, add the tomatoes, toss through and serve in a beautiful glass bowl.

Serves 6.

a safe journey

This gold Buddha (top) is in Kaluthara and is an icon in Sri Lanka. No truck driver or family on vacation would pass this spot without giving their spare coins as a donation; they hope this will protect them on their journey. Sri Lankans believe if you pass without making a donation, you could have bad luck.

Below is the Buddha at Dambulla near Kandalama in the Hill Country. This roadside temple can be seen from afar and is especially picturesque when the morning sun shines upon it.

art of the temple

The arts and crafts at my village temple in Ehliyagoda were created about 50 years ago when my grandfather invited an artist from the south to do the work. The temple was lit by coconut oil-fuelled clay lamps and whenever I went there I felt a sense of calm. This was a place I always visited when I needed an escape from the world, especially when I was upset, a place I could relax and look at the beautiful artwork and sculptures.

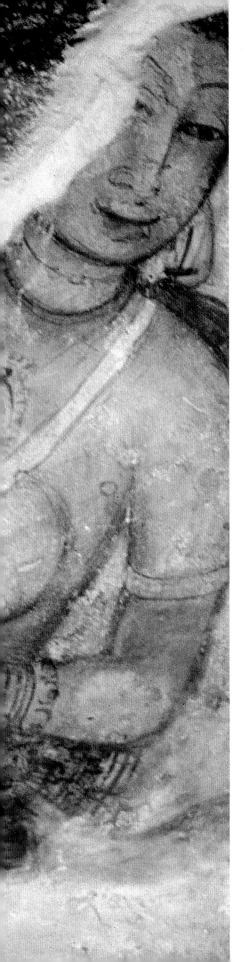

Date chutney

2½ cups white vinegar

3 cups sugar

500 g (1 lb 2 oz) pitted dates

4 teaspoons crushed garlic

3 teaspoons crushed ginger

2 teaspoons ground mustard
seeds

1 teaspoon mixed spices

1 tablespoon chilli powder

2 teaspoons salt

1 cup sultanas

salt to taste

Put the vinegar and sugar in a pan over low heat and heat for about 2½ minutes, until the sugar is dissolved. Add the rest of the ingredients except sultanas and salt. Cook for about 25 minutes, stirring occasionally, until mixture is thick but not gluggy.

Remove from heat; add sultanas and salt to taste. Leave to cool. Store and seal in sterilised bottles.

This teams well with hot curries, especially fish curries, and Dried Pork Curry.

Makes about two jars, serves about 20.

Eggplant pickle

This is another lovely dish, which can be served with coconut milk-based curries. It's a festive dish to be served on grand occasions.

500 g (1 lb 2 oz) eggplants
   (aubergines) – about 2–3
oil for frying
2 onions
2 green chillies
extra oil for deep-frying
¼ cup coconut milk
1 teaspoon brown mustard seeds
½ teaspoon ground turmeric

1 cinnamon stick
10 curry leaves (or 2 bay leaves)
1 tomato, chopped
1 teaspoon ground chilli
1 tablespoon sugar
1 tablespoon white vinegar
1 teaspoon salt

Cut eggplants in half and then cut into thin strips lengthways.

Heat oil in a pan and place eggplant in pan in batches and fry until golden brown – about 3 minutes. Take care not to overcrowd the pan. Remove eggplant from pan and place on absorbent paper in a colander. Drain.

Peel and cut the onions into quarters. Cut the chillies in half across the middle then slice in half lengthways. Deep-fry onion and chillies then drain them on absorbent paper.

Place coconut milk in a pan on medium heat. Add the mustard seeds, turmeric, cinnamon, curry leaves, tomato and ground chilli. Bring to boil, reduce heat and simmer for 5 minutes. Add eggplant, onion and chillies to pan.

Stir through, then reduce heat. Add sugar, vinegar and salt, stir and cook for a further 2 minutes. Remove from heat.

Serve with meat dishes, like a relish.

Serves about 10 –12.

Lunu dehi
tomato and lime pickles

This is hard to stop eating. It has a great sweet and sour chilli kick - like a relish - is perfect with meat dishes, or as a spread for roast beef, and is lovely with fish - try it on grilled fish or in a tuna sandwich. You can buy the lime pickle base in supermarkets.

350 g (12 oz) lime pickle

2 tomatoes, deseeded and finely chopped

1 onion, finely chopped

1½ tablespoons sweet paprika

4 tablespoons sugar

1 tablespoon salt

Add all ingredients together and mix.
Serve. That's it.

Serves 20.

an executive kitchen

My grandmother's kitchen was my second home, the place where I spent my weekends and holidays. Because my grandfather was head of the village, the house was a meeting point for the community, which meant the kitchen was a hive of activity and the kitchen was often overflowing with food and people.

There were four to five small fires on a brick bench, which had firewood stored underneath and above it. Clay pots covered in charcoal – the result of generation after generation of cooking – were stacked against the walls. Spicy, aromatic curries were cooked in those pots. Clay-pot cooking with firewood is unique; it is difficult to recreate the flavours that result in a commercial kitchen with stainless steel pans.

Huge glass jars with aluminium tops stood on the shelves, full of cardamom, curry powder and cloves. Dried fish hung from the ceiling. Sambols were made using huge mortars and pestles. Chutneys and pickles were mixed by women sitting on low stools. And outside in the lush garden grew curry leaf plants, lime trees, pepper and coffee plants, while red rice was delivered straight from the surrounding paddies.

Four or five people would be working at a time in the kitchen and visitors would often come bearing gifts of sweetmeats and seafood. Much food was prepared: not just for my grandparents, but for the families of the people who worked in the kitchen. More food was always on hand in case there was a shortage at the village temple for the monks, or as is tradition in Sri Lanka, for strangers or family members who might drop in unannounced.

If a comparison could be drawn between my grandmother's kitchen and a busy restaurant in a Western city, she was like the executive chief, giving directions, tasting and putting the final finishing touches to a dish.

Kangkung
tempered water spinach

1 bunch kangkung – water
  spinach (about 350 g/12 oz)
1 tablespoon oil
½ cup sliced onion
1 green chilli, sliced
1 tomato, diced
¼ teaspoon crushed dried chilli
¼ teaspoon salt

Break the stems off the water spinach and discard.

Heat the oil in a shallow pan over medium heat and add onion, green chilli and tomato. Cook until golden brown – about 1 minute. Increase heat to high, add kangkung, crushed chilli and salt, and quickly stir-fry, tossing until leaves are cooked but still hold their shape.

Serves 4–6.

Tip
The pan must be very hot or the spinach will wilt.

Variation
Any of your favourite leafy greens can be prepared in the same style.

In Sri Lanka they sell bananas by the flower – still attached to the stem – at wholesale markets. In every village, most houses have a banana tree growing at the back of the garden. It is up to the young man of the house to cut down the flower when it is still green and take the bananas to market.

Raita
cucumber and yoghurt

This dish can be served with any hot curry and your guests will be very happy. It has a soothing effect and balances the chilli and spice flavours of curries.

1 cucumber (about 225 g/8 oz),
  peeled, seeded and chopped
½ cup finely chopped onion
½ teaspoon chopped green chilli
1 cup plain non-fat yoghurt
½ teaspoon ground cumin
¼ teaspoon chilli powder
½ teaspoon salt
½ teaspoon sugar

Mix all ingredients together and place in the fridge for 10 minutes. Serve chilled.

Serves 4–6.

sri lankan service

Dried fish and lentils are often bought from a small grocery shop on the roadside in a village. These little shops may also sell tea, savoury snacks, clothes and sarongs. The goods are wrapped in the village newspaper and tied up with a tiny string.

When we bought something, the young girl serving at the stall usually offered a little bit of information and advice – she would tell you who had been buying her goods and what was freshest. She would then wrap the goods in newspaper and tie them up with string.

In the Western world such service would be a luxury, but for us it wasn't – everyone wanted their purchases in plastic bags and self-service. Progress is inevitable, but I hope it stays the old-fashioned way in my village.

wild bounty

meat, fish and poultry

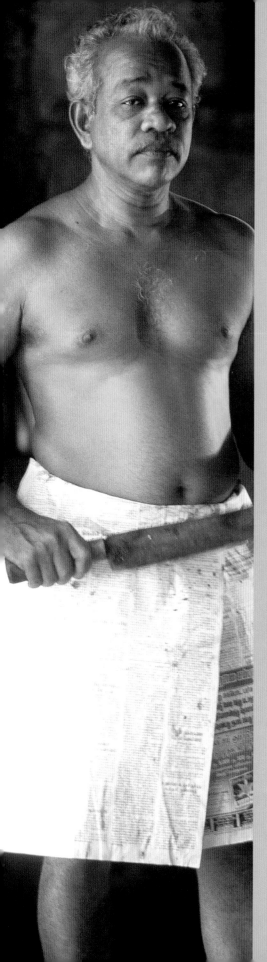

Curries are the most famous and most prevalent of all Sri Lankan dishes. Despite the fact that there is such an infinite variety of curries, the more one becomes familiar with Sri Lankan food, the more one sees there are categories of curries to which each different dish belongs.

Curries owe their character to the freshly ground spices for which Sri Lanka is so famous - coriander, cardamom, cumin and chilli. Curry leaves also play an important part in the flavour and it is believed they help counteract the cholesterol in the coconut oil traditionally used by Sri Lankans.

Curries are an amalgam of ingredients in which individual flavours are not easily distinguished. From meat and poultry to seafood and vegetable-based versions highlighting jackfruit, pumpkin or sweet potato, Sri Lankan curries offer an endless array of possibilities that will never cease to stimulate and inspire.

At the table they are mixed with rice, sambols, chutneys or pickles, together with bread, hoppers or broken pappadams. If a curry proves to be too hot, eat some more rice or bread with it; water will only accentuate the burning sensation.

And remember, try mixing everything and eating with your fingers - you'll be surprised what a difference it can make.

A fishmonger in a Colombo market
preparing the day's catch.

Lamb baduma with coriander leaves

This is a Sri Lankan equivalent of a South East Asian stir-fry.

2 tablespoons coconut oil
  or vegetable oil

½ teaspoon fenugreek

10 cm (4 in) piece of rampe
  (pandanus leaf)

10 curry leaves

2 cups thinly sliced onion –
  about 3 onions

1 teaspoon minced garlic

1 teaspoon minced ginger

1 green chilli, thinly sliced

500 g (1 lb 2 oz) lamb,
  in thin strips

1 teaspoon salt

1 teaspoon ground black pepper

1 tablespoon lemon juice

½ cup chopped coriander
  (cilantro) leaves

Spice mixture

1 tablespoon Roasted Curry
  Powder (see page 74)

½ teaspoon sweet paprika

¼ teaspoon ground turmeric

¼ teaspoon chilli powder

2 tablespoons water

Mix spices with water to form a paste. Set aside.

Add oil to a pan over medium heat. Add fenugreek, rampe and curry leaves and cook for 20 seconds. Add the onion, garlic, ginger and chilli and sauté for 2 minutes until golden brown. Add the spice paste to the pan, stir thoroughly and cook until the spices release aromatic aromas – about 5 minutes. Add lamb, salt and pepper and sauté until lamb is cooked and tender, stirring continuously – about 15–20 minutes.

Stir through lemon juice and coriander (cilantro) leaves. Remove from heat and serve with roti, bread or rice, or a vegetable curry.

Serves 4–6.

Dried pork curry

In Sri Lanka, we cook pork with the fat on, for flavour, but it's not advisable these days for those who are health conscious.

2 tablespoons oil

½ cinnamon stick

10 cm (4 in) piece of rampe (pandanus leaf)

¼ teaspoon fenugreek

10 curry leaves

1 onion, chopped

5 cm (2 in) piece of lemongrass, bruised

2 teaspoons crushed garlic

1 teaspoon crushed ginger

1 teaspoon chilli powder

1 tablespoon Roasted Curry Powder (see page 74)

1 teaspoon sweet paprika

¼ teaspoon ground turmeric

2 tablespoons tomato paste

1 cup chopped or canned tomatoes

1 kg (2 lb 3 oz) lean pork, cut into 2 cm (¾ in) cubes

2 cups water

2 teaspoons salt

1½ teaspoons ground black pepper

Paste

1 tablespoon rice

1 tablespoon desiccated (shredded) coconut

½ teaspoon mustard seeds

2 tablespoons white vinegar

To make paste, brown rice in a dry pan over low heat until golden – about 2 minutes. Add coconut and mustard seeds and brown for about 15–20 seconds, tossing continuously so as not to burn. Remove from heat and place in a food processor with vinegar and blend into a paste (this can also be done using a mortar and pestle). Set aside.

Heat the oil in a pan over medium heat. Add the cinnamon, rampe, fenugreek, curry leaves and cook until brown – about 30 seconds. Add the onion, lemongrass, garlic and ginger and sauté for a further 4 minutes. Add the chilli powder, roasted curry powder, sweet paprika, turmeric, tomato paste and tomatoes and cook for another 2 minutes, stirring occasionally.

Add the meat, stir well to mix through the spices and sauté for 3 minutes. Add water, salt and pepper and mix thoroughly. Bring to the boil and cook for 15 minutes then reduce heat and simmer for 30 minutes.

Add coconut-rice paste and cook for a further 6–7 minutes, stirring occasionally, until liquid has reduced. Take care not to burn the dish or the bottom of the pan.

Serves 4.

Mutton curry

750 g (1 lb 10 oz) lean mutton, cubed

Marinade

1 teaspoon freshly ground black pepper

½ teaspoon sweet paprika or chilli powder

1 tablespoon oil

2 tablespoons tomato paste

½ teaspoon salt

½ teaspoon ground turmeric

2 cloves garlic, crushed

1 teaspoon chopped ginger

Tempering spices

2 tablespoons oil

¼ teaspoon fenugreek (optional)

10 cm (4 in) piece of rampe (pandanus leaf)

10 curry leaves, fresh or dried, (or 2 bay leaves)

1 onion, chopped

½ cinnamon stick

2 cloves

2 cardamom pods

5 cm (2 in) piece of lemongrass, bruised

½ teaspoon sweet paprika

1 teaspoon Roasted Curry Powder (see page 74)

3½ cups mutton stock (see page 63) or 4 cups beef stock

½ cup coconut milk

salt and pepper to taste

½ cup chopped coriander (cilantro) leaves

Combined all marinade ingredients and cover mutton with mixture; place in the fridge and marinate for 1 hour.

Heat oil in a pot on medium heat. Add fenugreek and sauté for 10 seconds. Add the rampe and cook for 30 seconds. Add curry leaves and onion and cook until onion has caramelised – about 2 minutes. Add the rest of the tempering ingredients and cook for 1½ minutes, making sure not to burn the paprika. Add the meat, without burning the curry powders. Toss over heat for a couple of minutes to seal the meat cubes then cover the pan and cook for about 10 minutes.

Add the stock slowly, a cup at a time. Cook for 3–6 minutes, making sure liquid is absorbed before adding another cup of stock. After a couple of ladlefuls of stock have been absorbed and reduced, cover the meat with the remaining stock. Simmer for about 45–50 minutes.

Add coconut milk and more stock at the end if you prefer more gravy. Simmer for 4–5 minutes. Check seasoning and add salt and pepper if required. Sprinkle coriander leaves on top and serve with steamed rice or bread.

Serves 4.

Variation

This curry can also be made using goat meat.

Mutton stock

3.5 kg (7 lb) mutton bones
2 tablespoons oil
1 onion, chopped
2 cloves garlic, chopped
1 stick celery, chopped
1 carrot, chopped
½ coriander (cilantro) root, chopped
5 litres (10 pints) water

To make the mutton stock, first pre-heat oven to 200°C (400°F). Place mutton bones on an oven tray and roast in oven for 45 minutes, turning the bones occasionally.

Heat oil in a large pot, add onion, garlic, celery, carrot and coriander root and sauté for 3 minutes. Add mutton bones and water and bring to the boil, skimming occasionally. Simmer for 2 hours. You may reduce further for a more intense flavour. You should end up with about 2 litres (4 pints) stock.

Chicken curry

8–12 chicken drumsticks

1 teaspoon chilli powder

2 tablespoons Roasted Curry Powder (see page 74)

1½ teaspoons ground turmeric

2–3 teaspoons salt

4 tablespoons vegetable oil

2 onions, sliced

5 cm (2 in) piece of rampe (pandanus leaf)

10 curry leaves (or 2 bay leaves)

1 cinnamon stick

6 cardamom pods

40 g (1½ oz) lemongrass, white part only, chopped

1–2 green chillies, chopped

2 teaspoons crushed ginger

2 cloves garlic, crushed

6 tomatoes, chopped

1 teaspoon freshly ground black pepper

300 ml (10 fl oz) coconut milk

½ cup coriander (cilantro) leaves, chopped

Season the chicken with chilli powder, curry powder, turmeric and salt and leave for 30 minutes.

Heat oil in a pan until very hot. Add onions, rampe, curry leaves, cinnamon, cardamom, lemongrass, green chilli, ginger and garlic and sauté until golden brown – 3–4 minutes. Add the tomato and cook for 2 minutes. Then add the chicken and pepper and sauté for 6 minutes.

Add the coconut milk and bring to the boil. Simmer for 15–20 minutes or until the chicken is cooked. Sprinkle with coriander (cilantro) leaves and serve.

Serves 4.

Chicken curry in a hurry

2 tablespoons oil

1 cinnamon stick

10 curry leaves (or 2 bay leaves)

1 clove garlic, crushed

1 teaspoon ginger, chopped

1 cardamom pod, bruised

1 clove, bruised

2 onions, chopped

1 teaspoon sweet paprika

½ teaspoon chilli powder (optional)

¼ teaspoon ground turmeric

1 teaspoon Roasted Curry Powder (see page 74)

2 tablespoons tomato paste

1 cup chopped or canned tomatoes

1 chicken, cut into 8–12 pieces or 1 kg (2 lb 3 oz) chicken breast fillets or maryland (thigh and leg) fillets

5 cups water or chicken stock

½ cup coconut milk

1 teaspoon salt

½ teaspoon freshly ground black pepper

½ cup chopped coriander (cilantro) leaves

Heat oil in a pan over medium heat. Add the cinnamon, curry leaves, garlic, ginger, cardamom and clove and cook for 30 seconds without burning. Add the onion and sauté until golden brown – about 2 minutes.

Add the paprika, chilli powder, turmeric, curry powder, tomato paste and tomatoes and cook for a further minute. Add the chicken and cook for 3 minutes, stirring until chicken is brown. Add water or chicken stock to cover the pieces. Cook until meat is tender – for breast this will be about 8 minutes. Add coconut milk and bring to the boil. Remove from heat, check seasoning and add salt and pepper to taste (you won't need much salt if you used chicken stock).

Serve sprinkled with chopped coriander (cilantro) and steamed rice.

Serves 4.

Beef curry with potatoes

500 g (1 lb 2 oz) lean beef, cubed

2 potatoes, peeled and cubed

2 tablespoons oil

¼ teaspoon fenugreek

1 onion, chopped

10 curry leaves (or 2 bay leaves)

½ cinnamon stick

1 teaspoon freshly ground black pepper

5 cm (2 in) piece of rampe (pandanus leaf)

5 cm (2 in) piece of lemongrass, bruised

1 cup chopped or canned tomatoes

1 cup thick coconut milk

3 cups water

Marinade

½ cup white vinegar

1 teaspoon Roasted Curry Powder (see recipe page 74)

1½ tablespoons salt

2 cloves garlic, crushed

2 teaspoons fresh ginger, crushed

1 teaspoon ground mustard seeds

1 teaspoon sweet paprika

½ teaspoon chilli powder

½ teaspoon ground turmeric

Mix together all marinade ingredients. Marinate beef in this for 1 hour in the fridge.

Place potatoes in a pot and boil for about 10 minutes until potatoes are soft but still firm. Drain and set aside.

Heat oil in a medium pan on medium heat. Add fenugreek and cook for about 20 seconds. Add onion, curry leaves, cinnamon, pepper, rampe and lemongrass and sauté until onion is caramelised – about 1 minute. Drain meat from marinade and set marinade aside. Add meat to the pan and sauté, tossing, until meat is sealed and brown – about 7 minutes. Add the marinade liquid, tomatoes, coconut milk and water and cook over low heat until beef is tender – about 1 hour.

Once the meat is tender, stir in potatoes and mix through. Serve with rice or bread.

Serves 4.

Tip

Like all good curries, this dish tastes better if kept overnight in the fridge and reheated.

beneath the surface

During my school holidays I used to go to the gem pits that belonged to my grandmother and work in the role of *kumtheruwa* – a supervisor. My grandmother would never appear herself at the gem pits, so I would go, being given a huge umbrella to keep the sun off my skin.

People who worked in the gem pits would make me a seat so I could overlook the work from a safe distance. I must say I didn't have a clue what was going on in the pits - the workers could have taken all the gems they found each day for all I knew - but I pretended I knew what was going on down there.

This was how I earned my school holiday money – I was always given a share of the profits as payment for the work I did, so I used to pray the men would find gems. The workers would start as the sun rose – about 6.30 a.m. – and they would work until 4.30 or 5 p.m., when they would come for a final cup of tea before going home.

Up to four people at a time would work in the gem pits, using traditional methods of mining: digging a tunnel, pumping water out of the pit and sifting through the gravel. The men often worked for weeks before they found anything, following lines or seams of gravel which they hoped held the gems. The greatest prizes were precious stones: a sapphire or a ruby. Other gems found in Sri Lankan mines include cat's eye, alexandrite, quartz, garnets and topaz.

I loved my days at the gem pits. Early in the morning the workers' wives would bring them a kettle of tea and seasoned coconut shells from which to drink the tea, which was sweetened with palm sugar placed on their palm. Out there beside the pits I knew no one was watching me and I used to join them for a tea break.

Later breakfast would come out to us, sent by my grandmother. A girl would arrive with a basket made of palm leaves on her head in which she carried the meal. She would have yams boiled and wrapped in banana leaves, and chilli sambols with dried fish. Breakfast would end with a nice cup of tea in a coconut shell with jaggary – palm sugar – which used to make my day perfect.

The next meal would arrive at 12.30 – red rice, sambols, pickles, vegetable curries, and a meat curry of the day – chicken one day, fish the next – followed by fruit – a banana or mango – or sweetmeat, depending on what the women had been preparing in my grandmother's kitchen that day.

After meals, the workers would take the equivalent of a cigarette break and chew betel leaves with tobacco, which made their teeth go red.

"Up to four people at a time would work in the gem pits, using traditional methods of mining: digging a tunnel, pumping water out of the pit and sifting through the gravel. The men often worked for weeks before they found anything, following lines or seams of gravel which they hoped held the gems."

This is a roadside eating place for low-earning labourers, such as day workers who carry huge bags of flour from trucks to storage or those who work at the port. The café is rough – there are no tablecloths, just sheets of newspaper and when you leave the waiter throws them out and places a clean sheet on the table. The serviettes are also made from newspapers and the food is served on rough stainless steel plates, which are the simplest form of crockery. Lunch at such a cafe costs about 5 rupees – about 2 or 3 cents and consists of a lentil curry or a dry fish curry with a coconut sauce served with pieces of bread broken off from a loaf and strong tea in a glass with sugar.

Curry powder

In the past, my grandmother used to prepare curry powder daily, using whole ingredients that were either roasted or sun-dried before grinding. If they were being roasted, each ingredient in turn was heated in a pan until its desired colour was reached – light, dark or very dark. The end result could vary between mild or pronounced curry powder aromas, which filled the house each day. The mixed spices were then ground in a mortar and pestle and the women who worked in the kitchen would use these blends to prepare the meals.

Curry blends

My mother stressed that the order in which each ingredient was placed in the pan for roasting was essential. The biggest ingredients are added first to roast through – chilli, coriander seeds, cardamom pods, cinnamon stick – while ingredients such as fenugreek and turmeric are added last so as not to burn them. This is the secret of fine curry powder.

Each and every house in a village will make a slightly different blend of curry powder, but my mum always said the secret is in the spices.

When the mixture was right, the aroma of the roasting spices could be smelt in neighbouring villages. And when the aroma was right, I always used to wish I could join the family making that blend for lunch.

In the village today, they still make curry powder by hand rather than buying it from the shops. My mother would grind the spices with coconut, using a grinding stone and adding water to the bowl. She would keep the ball of moist curry powder in the fridge for use. You should keep curry powders in an airtight container in a cool, dry place, or in the fridge, as you would fresh coffee.

Roasted curry powders are ideal for meat curries, while unroasted powder suits vegetable curries. But this is a rule that can be broken.

For vegetarians, cook with roasted curry powders as it will produce a stronger flavour in the absence of meat flavouring. You should also use roasted curry powders in soya curries.

recipes on following pages

Curry powder

Nutmeg is the hard seed of a tropical fruit grown throughout Sri Lanka. The dried seed is grated or ground and used in curries as well as drinks and desserts.

Roasted curry powder

This is the blend used for meat dishes.

6 cm (2½ in) stalk of lemongrass, white part only

1 stick cinnamon

½ cup coriander seeds

10 curry leaves

10 cm (4 in) piece of rampe (pandanus leaf), cut into four pieces

2 cardamom pods

3 cloves

¼ cup cumin seeds

¼ cup fennel seeds

Place lemongrass and cinnamon stick in a pan on medium heat and toss gently, roasting until golden brown – about three minutes. Then add coriander seeds, curry leaves, rampe, cardamom and cloves and brown for a further minute. Remove from heat and add cumin and fennel and toss through the other ingredients. These cook with the heat of the pan. Place in a food processor and blend until reduced to a powder, or you can grind ingredients with a mortar and pestle.

Variation

You can add dry red chilli powder, or include dry red chilli in the roasting pan, and roast until slightly golden brown. Keep this blend separate from the one without chilli and use in curries as required.

Vegetable curry powder (unroasted)

⅛ cup rice

¼ cup desiccated (shredded)
   coconut

¼ cup ground coriander

⅛ cup ground cumin

¼ cup ground fennel

½ tablespoon ground fenugreek

10 curry leaves

½ teaspoon ground turmeric

Toss rice in a warm pan until lightly brown – about 2 minutes. Add coconut and shake in pan until golden – about 30 seconds.

Remove from the pan, place in a small food processor with the rest of the ingredients and blend to a powder. This can also be done using a mortar and pestle or a coffee grinder.

Even though this is an unroasted curry powder, my mother always warmed the other ingredients – coriander, cumin, etc. – to release their flavours. It also makes them easier to pound.

Variations

● You can include a 5 cm (2 in) piece of rampe (pandanus leaf) and the white part of 1 stalk of lemongrass.

● My mother would add 2 cloves garlic and a 3 cm (1¼ in) piece of ginger, sliced.

Aromatic spice blend

This is a simple but beautiful spice blend which is used as a seasoning. It is ideal for vegetarian curries: before serving any of your favourite curries, sprinkle this aromatic blend on top and toss.

½ cup cumin seeds

1 cinnamon stick

3 cardamom pods

3 cloves

Add all ingredients together and roast in a warm pan, tossing gently until ingredients are a coffee colour but not burnt. Grind ingredients with a mortar and pestle or coffee grinder.

Variation

This is another aromatic blend, which is prepared in the same way as the blend above.

⅓ cup fennel cumin

⅓ cup cumin

6 cardamom pods

1 clove

5 coriander seeds

¼ teaspoon fenugreek

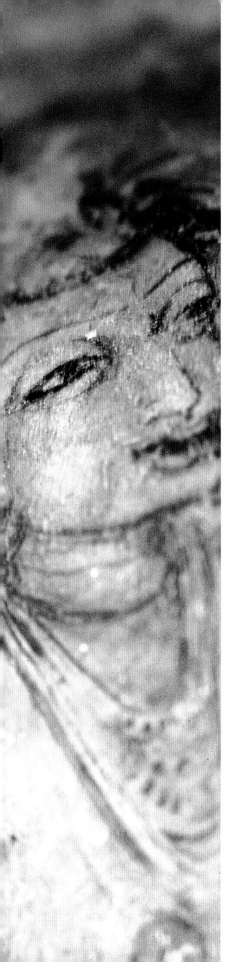

Devilled chicken

900 g (2 lb) boneless, skinless, chicken thighs, cut into 4 cm (1½ in) pieces

¼ teaspoon ground turmeric

1 teaspoon salt

3 tablespoons oil

2 onions, quartered

1 teaspoon crushed garlic

1 teaspoon crushed ginger

2 capsicums (bell peppers), red or green, cut into 3 cm (1¼ in) pieces

½ teaspoon ground black pepper

1 tablespoon tomato paste

juice of 1 lemon

Coat chicken cubes in turmeric and salt. Place 2 tablespoons of oil in a pan over medium heat, add chicken and cook, stirring, until meat is sealed – about 10 minutes. Remove chicken from pan and set aside.

Add remaining oil to pan, then add onion, garlic and ginger and cook for 1 minute. Add the capsicum (bell pepper), pepper and tomato paste and return meat to pan. Stir-fry for 1 minute. Remove from heat and add lemon juice.

Serve with roti or as a snack.

Serves 4 – 6.

Prawn curry

1 tablespoon vegetable oil

¼ teaspoon fenugreek

¼ cup diced onion

½ cinnamon stick

10 cm (4 in) piece of rampe (pandanus leaf)

8 curry leaves (or 1 bay leaf)

½ teaspoon crushed ginger

½ teaspoon crushed garlic

1 cup diced or canned tomatoes

¼ teaspoon ground turmeric

¼ teaspoon chilli powder

½ teaspoon sweet paprika

1 teaspoon curry powder

¼ teaspoon ground mustard seeds

1 teaspoon salt

750 g (1 lb 10 oz) green prawns, shelled and deveined

½ cup water

¾ cup coconut milk

1 tablespoon lemon juice

Heat oil in a pan over medium heat. Add fenugreek, onion, cinnamon, rampe, curry leaves, ginger and garlic and cook until golden brown – about 1 minute. Add the tomatoes, turmeric, chilli powder, paprika, curry powder, ground mustard seeds and salt, and cook for another 2–3 minutes.

Add the prawns, stir vigorously and cook for a minute, stirring continuously. Add water, cover and bring to boil. Cook until prawns are opaque. Remove lid, add coconut milk, stir through and return to the boil briefly.

Remove from heat, add the lemon juice and stir through. Leave to stand for a minute or two before serving, accompanied by rice.

Serves 4.

Dhallo curry
squid curry

1 tablespoon rice

1 tablespoon desiccated (shredded) coconut

2 tablespoons vegetable oil

2 onions, chopped

10 cm (4 in) piece of rampe (pandanus leaf)

10 curry leaves

¼ teaspoon fenugreek

½ cinnamon stick

1 teaspoon crushed ginger

1 teaspoon crushed garlic

½ cup chopped or canned tomatoes

½ teaspoon chilli powder

½ teaspoon paprika

1 teaspoon ground black pepper

¼ teaspoon ground turmeric

1 teaspoon Roasted Curry Powder (see page 74)

1 teaspoon salt

2 pieces of goraka (optional)

650 g (1½ lb) cleaned squid, cut into rings

3 cups water

Roast rice in a dry pan over low heat until golden – about 2 minutes. Add coconut, stir through and roast for another 20 seconds. Grind into a paste with a mortar and pestle. Set aside.

Heat the oil in a pan over medium heat. Add the onion, rampe, curry leaves, fenugreek, cinnamon, ginger and garlic and cook until golden brown – about 2 minutes. Add the tomatoes, chilli powder, paprika, pepper, turmeric, curry powder, salt and goraka and cook for a further 1–2 minutes until ingredients are mixed thoroughly.

Add the squid, stir through for about 1 minute. Add the water and coconut-rice paste and bring to boil. Cover and cook for 40–45 minutes.

Serve with lashings of lovely red rice, a hot sambol or a white vegetable curry. Leftovers can be kept in the fridge and eaten with roti or bread the next day.

Serves 4.

Tip

In Sri Lanka we cook squid for a long time, about 40–45 minutes. Some people believe cooking squid for a long time makes it tough, but this is only true for squid cooked for a little longer than 5 minutes. If cooked for long enough, squid loses this rubbery texture and becomes tender again.

Prawns tempered

This recipe is from Kandalama, one of Sri Lanka's most beautiful hotels.

900 g (2 lb) green prawns
1 teaspoon salt
juice of ½ a lime
2 tablespoons oil
1 teaspoon crushed garlic
1 teaspoon crushed ginger
10 curry leaves
2 onions, sliced into rings
1 green chilli, sliced thinly

1 red capsicum (bell pepper),
cut into 3 cm (1¼ in) pieces
1 green capsicum (bell pepper),
cut into 3 cm (1¼ in) pieces
1 tablespoon chilli sauce
1 tablespoon tomato paste
1 tablespoon mango chutney
salt and pepper to taste
lime juice to taste

Remove heads from prawns, shell, devein and wash, leaving the tails on. Place the prawns in a dish with salt and lime juice, mix thoroughly and leave in the fridge for 30 minutes.

Put oil in wok over high heat and add garlic, ginger and curry leaves and cook for 30 seconds. Add the prawns and stir until prawns are opaque – about 1 minute. Remove prawns from the wok and set aside. Add onion to wok, then chilli and capsicum (bell pepper) and toss for 2 minutes. Add chilli sauce, tomato paste and chutney then return prawns and cook for 2–3 minutes.

Taste and add salt, pepper or a splash of lime juice if needed and serve with steamed rice.

Serves 4.

Blue swimmer crab and sweet chilli

This recipe comes from the Colombo Hilton where I worked as a first commis, a role training chefs take before they qualify.

2 blue swimmer crabs
pinch of salt and pepper
juice of ½ a lime
oil for deep frying
extra 1 tablespoon oil
1 onion, chopped
10 cm (4 in) piece of rampe (pandanus leaf) (optional)
10 curry leaves
1 teaspoon crushed garlic
1 teaspoon crushed ginger

1 stalk lemongrass, white part only, bruised
1 teaspoon Roasted Curry Powder (see page 74)
½ teaspoon ground black pepper
½ teaspoon dried chilli flakes
1 tablespoon tomato paste
1 tablespoon sweet chilli sauce
½ cup fish stock or water
½ teaspoon sugar

Remove the shells from the crabs. Discard fibrous tissue and wash under running water. Break crab in half down the middle with legs still attached to each half.

Season crabmeat with salt, pepper and lime juice and deep-fry in a hot pot for about 5 minutes, until crab is red. Place on absorbent paper and drain off excess oil.

In a pan, heat 1 tablespoon oil over medium heat, add onion, rampe and curry leaves and cook until golden brown – about 2–3 minutes. Add garlic, ginger and lemongrass and cook for a further minute. Add curry powder, pepper and chilli flakes and cook for another minute. Add tomato paste and chilli sauce, then fish stock and sugar. Stir thoroughly.

Place crabs in a large bowl, pour sauce over, toss and serve.

You can't eat a crab with a knife and fork so this dish has to be enjoyed with your fingers. Remember to place fingerbowls of warm water with a wedge of lemon or lime on the table, to wash your hands after you have eaten the crab.

Serves 2.

Mirus malu

This is a traditional hot fish curry.

2 tablespoons oil

2 pieces of goraka (optional)

½ cup chopped onion

10 cm (4 in) piece of rampe
(pandanus leaf)

¼ teaspoon fenugreek

8 curry leaves

½ cinnamon stick

1 teaspoon crushed garlic

1 teaspoon crushed ginger

½ cup chopped or canned
tomatoes

2 cups water

750 g (1 lb 10 oz) tuna, cubed,
washed and drained

salt to taste

1 tablespoon lemon juice

Spice paste

1 teaspoon freshly ground
black pepper

1 teaspoon salt

1 tablespoon chilli powder or
½ teaspoon chilli powder plus
1½ teaspoons sweet paprika

1 tablespoon water

To make spice paste, grind all ingredients together using a mortar and pestle. Set aside.

Heat oil in a pan over medium heat. Wash the goraka and add to the pan with the onion, rampe, fenugreek, curry leaves, cinnamon, garlic, ginger and tomatoes and cook until golden brown – about 2–3 minutes.

Add the spice paste slowly, while stirring. Cook for 1 minute. Add water and bring to the boil. Add the fish, turn heat down until liquid is simmering and cook until fish is opaque – about 10–15 minutes. Add extra water if needed, to ensure fish is covered. Stir liquid occasionally but try not to break the fish. Check flavours and add salt if needed.

Remove from heat and add lemon juice. Serve with boiled rice or bread, and sambols.

Serves 4.

Thoramalu
fish curry

500 g (1 lb 2 oz) white fish such as spanish mackerel

170 ml (6 fl oz) light coconut milk or 20 g (¾ oz) coconut powder and 170 ml (6 fl oz) water

3 green chillies

½ teaspoon fenugreek, soaked in water for 30 minutes

10 curry leaves

5 cm (2 in) piece of lemongrass, bruised

1 onion, chopped

1 tomato, chopped

1 tablespoon tomato paste

2 teaspoons salt

1 tablespoon unroasted curry powder

½ teaspoon saffron or turmeric powder

60 ml (2 fl oz) full-cream coconut milk or 20 g (¾ oz) coconut powder and 60 ml (2 fl oz) water

Cut the fish into 3 cm cubes. Set aside.

Place light coconut milk in a pot over medium heat with all the other ingredients except the fish and the full-cream coconut milk. Mix all ingredients, bring to boil, stirring well.

When liquid is boiling, add fish. Lower temperature and simmer until the fish is cooked – about 5 minutes. Add the coconut milk, bring to boil, then take off the heat immediately.

Serves 6.

Tip

Do not stir the fish while it is in the pot, as the flesh will break up. Instead, shake the pot to mix ingredients.

Ambulthyial

This is a traditional fish curry from the southern part of Sri Lanka. The coast of Sri Lanka has an abundance of fish in season. This dish has a pickled flavour and is made using goraka, also known as gamboge, a segmented fruit whose sour taste is similar to tamarind; it is available in dried form in Asian grocery stores.

8–10 pieces of goraka (gamboge)
650 g (1½ lb) fresh tuna, cubed
½ cinnamon stick
1 clove garlic
10 curry leaves
1 teaspoon ground black pepper
1 teaspoon salt

Soak goraka in 1 cup of warm water for 3 hours. Drain, wash and set aside.

Wash and drain the fish. Pat dry with a paper towel: the fish must be dry for this recipe. Set aside.

Place goraka, cinnamon, garlic, curry leaves, pepper and salt in a food processor and blend into a fine paste. Rub the fish with the paste and place the fish in a bowl, covered with plastic wrap, in the fridge for 30 minutes.

Place fish in a non-stick pan (or wipe some oil over the base of a pan) on medium-low heat, cover with a lid and cook for 35 minutes. Turn fish after 15 minutes. Shake pan occasionally, taking care not to break the fish.

Serve with hoppers, stringhoppers, coconut rice or plain rice.

Serves 4.

a moveable feast

Food is a moveable feast in Sri Lanka. Outside Colombo, the people buy their food on a daily basis from the local market or travelling salesmen, who bring their goods to town on the back of a bike or in a cart.

nature's harvest

vegetables

Many Sri Lankan villagers make a living attending to stalls, selling vegetables harvested fresh from their backyard patch. Some visit weekly markets to sell their produce, while others set up temporary stalls on the roads outside their homes each day, to catch workers and travellers passing by.

Drumstick – long fleshy pods that resemble beans but which grow on trees – are stacked on the stall shelves along with other Sri Lankan favourites – bitter gourd, snake gourd, jackfruit, okra, banana chillies and water spinach. Many other vegetables – cabbage, radishes, eggplant, tomatoes, yams, pumpkin, potatoes, carrots, beetroot, leeks and beans – are harvested throughout the year. All find their way at the peak of freshness to the markets, along with pulses such as chickpeas, red lentils and mung beans.

Vegetables are an integral part of the Sri Lankan diet. A popular way to start the day is a cup of porridge made with rice, coconut milk and the juice from leafy vegetables. At lunch vegetables are served in curries, sambols or in mallum, a leafy vegetable dish similar to a tabouli.

Dinner, the day's main meal, would never be served with meat and rice alone. There are always vegetables, which can range from a simple potato curry to a much more complex jackfruit curry.

The combinations of meat and vegetables are carefully chosen. A chicken curry matches perfectly with beetroot or okra curry and tempered dhal, while a lamb and coriander dish teams up with a snake bean curry. A dry goat curry is best when accompanied by a vegetable curry with a coconut base and a mallum, while a coconut milk-based fish curry is perfect when served with a lovely sautéed potato curry with chilli and coconut or a lentil and spinach dish.

Dhal with spinach

Dhal is a major part of a Sri Lankan everyday diet – no meal is cooked without it. My mother always used to add extra ingredients to dhal such as spinach, which enhances the lentil flavours and gives it visual appeal. Traditionally Sri Lankans eat dhal as a breakfast dish with bread or roti, but you can serve it as a lunch or light dinner or as an accompaniment for rice.

1 cup lentils

water for soaking

extra 2½ cups (750 ml) water

2 teaspoons coconut
   or vegetable oil

2 salted chillies (see page 101),
   broken into pieces

¼ teaspoon brown mustard seeds

5–10 curry leaves

½ onion, chopped

10 cm (4 in) piece of rampe
   (pandanus leaf) (optional)

2 cm (¾ in) piece of
   cinnamon stick

1 clove garlic, sliced

2 tomatoes, chopped

½ cup coconut milk

1 teaspoon salt

80 g (3 oz) baby spinach

Spice mixture

¼ teaspoon ground cumin

½ teaspoon ground coriander
   seeds

½ teaspoon sweet paprika

⅛ teaspoon ground turmeric

⅛ teaspoon chilli powder
   (optional)

¼ teaspoon fenugreek

1–2 cloves garlic, crushed

Cover lentils with water and soak for an hour. Drain and set aside.

Put the extra 2½ cups of water, the spice mixture and lentils into a saucepan and bring to the boil. Reduce heat and simmer uncovered for 5–6 minutes or until lentils are soft but not overcooked.

Heat the oil in a deep pan over medium heat. Add the salted chillies and mustard seeds and heat through until the mustard seeds pop up – about 30 seconds. Add the curry leaves, onion, rampe, cinnamon and garlic and cook for another 1–2 minutes, until the ingredients are brown but not burnt.

Add tomatoes and cook for another 2 minutes, stirring until the tomatoes are mixed well. Add lentil mixture, stir thoroughly and bring to the boil. Add coconut milk and salt, reduce heat and allow to simmer.

Remove from the heat, add spinach to mixture, stir through and serve.

Serves 4.

Ma-karal
snake bean curry

If you can't find snake beans, you can substitute green beans or yellow beans.

500 g (1 lb 2 oz) snake beans

3 tablespoons coconut oil or olive oil

1 onion, thinly sliced

10 curry leaves (or 2 bay leaves)

10 cm (4 in) piece of rampe (pandanus leaf)

1 tomato, cut into quarters

2 green chillies

1 teaspoon dried chilli flakes

1½ teaspoons ground coriander

¼ teaspoon fenugreek

½ teaspoon ground turmeric

1 teaspoon salt

1 tablespoon Maldive fish flakes (optional)

½ cup coconut milk

¼ teaspoon Roasted Curry Powder (optional) (see page 74)

String the beans, wash and cut into 3 cm (1½ in) pieces.

Heat oil in a pan over medium heat and add onion, curry leaves and rampe. Add the rest of the ingredients apart from the coconut milk and roasted curry powder and toss for a few minutes.

Add the coconut milk, bring to the boil and simmer until cooked through, about 7 minutes. Taste and sprinkle with the roasted curry powder if desired.

Like the okra curry, the beans are best undercooked — left with a bit of crunch.

Serves 4.

Chickpea curry

I like this chickpea curry – and it is a good source of many vitamins and calcium. If you are on a vegetarian diet, it is a perfect dish to give you extra energy.

2 cups chickpeas

water

1 stalk lemongrass, white part only

1 onion, chopped

3 green chillies, roughly chopped

3 cloves garlic, chopped

1 cup unsweetened coconut milk

extra ½ cup water, if needed

juice of ½ a lemon

½ cup chopped coriander (cilantro) leaves

Tempering spices

2 tablespoons oil

¼ teaspoon fenugreek

1 teaspoon dried red chilli flakes

1 cinnamon stick

¼ teaspoon mustard seeds

10 cm (4 in) piece of rampe (pandanus leaf)

10 curry leaves

½ teaspoon salt

1 cup chopped or canned tomatoes

Spice mix

½ teaspoon ground coriander

¼ teaspoon ground cumin

½ teaspoon chilli powder

1 teaspoon sweet paprika powder

¼ teaspoon ground turmeric

1 teaspoon Maldive fish flakes (optional)

Soak chickpeas in water overnight. Drain and place in a large pot over medium heat. Add enough water to cover and boil for 30–35 minutes, until they are soft.

Bruise the lemongrass with the back of a spoon. Chop roughly. Place onion, lemongrass, chilli and garlic in a food processor and blend into a fine paste.

Place tempering ingredients except tomatoes in a pan on medium heat and sauté until golden – about 30 seconds. Add tomatoes, lemongrass–onion paste and spice mix ingredients and cook for a further 3 minutes until mixture is coated thoroughly. Drain chickpeas, add to mixture and cook for a further 2 minutes. Add coconut milk and bring to the boil; also add the extra ½ cup of water if you prefer a runny sauce. Simmer for 3 minutes, stirring continuously so ingredients don't stick to pan.

Check seasoning, add salt if desired, remove from heat and add lemon juice. Sprinkle coriander (cilantro) on top and serve with Pol sambol (see recipe on page 37), roti or rice.

Serves 4.

Mango curry

This recipe comes from Senaka, the head chef at the Kandalama Hotel in Dambulla. One of the best hotels in Sri Lanka, it is renowned throughout the world for its international standards of environmental practices.

The chefs at the hotel produce dishes belonging to all the international cuisines, but their best is the selection of Sri Lankan dishes. I trained at Kandalama as a junior chef. Senaka was older than me and was a qualified chef when I was there, but he often gave me ideas for dishes.

1 mango
1 teaspoon mustard seeds
50 ml (2 fl oz) vinegar
1 tablespoon vegetable oil
½ onion, chopped finely
2 teaspoons crushed garlic

1 teaspoon crushed ginger
4–5 curry leaves
1 cinnamon stick
½ cup light coconut milk
½ cup thick coconut milk
salt to taste

Peel mango and cut into pieces lengthways.

Grind mustard seeds and vinegar together until they form a paste.

In a pan, heat oil over medium heat, add onion, garlic, ginger, curry leaves and cinnamon and sauté until onion is golden – about 2–3 minutes. Add mango, light coconut milk and mustard seed mixture and bring to the boil.

Reduce heat and simmer until mango is cooked and tender – about 3 minutes. Add thick coconut milk and simmer for a further 10 minutes. Taste and add salt if necessary.

This is a side dish to be served with meat and vegetable curries.

Serves 4.

This hut is at Kadugannawa - on the way to Kandy in the centre of Sri Lanka. Typically, a village family will live in a dwelling such as this; the front of the house is a stall from which they sell goods and they live at the back. The hut is made from bamboo and mud, which is cool in summer and warm in cooler weather. Behind the hut there will be a vegetable patch where the family grows the foods they sell. Among the offerings are coconuts, mangoes and butter fruit - avocado. Roadside vendors sell to people on pilgrimages to Kandy, to the Sacred Tooth Relic of the Buddha, and to bus and lorry drivers who stop for a break. Many also serve plain black tea with lots of sugar.

Themparaduwa

Themparaduwa is a thick spice mixture which gives extra flavour to dishes. It can be added to any curry just before serving: use about 1 tablespoon of the spicy onion mixture for four servings. While you don't eat the curry leaves, the cinnamon stick or the rampe, you should leave them in the mixture while you store it for continued flavour. This can be kept in an airtight container in the fridge for about a week.

5 tablespoons oil

2 medium onions, chopped

3–4 salted chillies (see page 101), broken into pieces

½ teaspoon mustard seeds

1 cinnamon stick

¼ teaspoon fenugreek

1 piece of rampe (pandanus leaf)

15 curry leaves

4 cloves garlic, sliced

1 teaspoon sweet paprika

Place oil in a pan over medium heat, add all ingredients and sauté until golden brown.

Tomato curry

2 tablespoons vegetable oil

¼ teaspoon fenugreek

¼ teaspoon brown mustard seeds

10 curry leaves

1 cinnamon stick

10 cm (4 in) piece of rampe (pandanus leaf) (optional)

1 onion, chopped

1 green chilli, chopped

500 g (1 lb 2 oz) medium tomatoes, quartered

1 cup unsweetened coconut milk

1 cup water

Spice mixture

½ teaspoon cumin seeds

1 teaspoon ground coriander

¼ teaspoon ground turmeric

1 teaspoon chilli powder, or sweet paprika for a milder sauce

1 teaspoon brown sugar

½ teaspoon salt (to taste)

2 teaspoons Maldive fish flakes (optional)

Heat the oil in a pan over medium heat. Add fenugreek, mustard seeds, curry leaves, cinnamon, rampe, onion and green chilli and cook until golden brown – about 2 minutes. Add spice mixture ingredients and cook for a further minute, being careful not to let mixture burn.

Add the tomatoes and cook for another 6–8 minutes, until they have softened. Add coconut milk and water, bring to the boil and simmer until the liquid thickens.

Serve as a side curry to a main vegetable, fish or meat curry with bread or rice.

Serves 4.

Mustard potatoes

Use your favourite potatoes, sweet potatoes or yams for this dish.

3–4 medium potatoes, peeled
and cut into 3 cm (1½ in) pieces

2 cups water

1 teaspoon salt

¼ teaspoon fenugreek

1 clove garlic, crushed

1 green chilli, chopped

1 cup chopped or canned
tomatoes

¼ teaspoon ground turmeric

½ teaspoon ground coriander

¼ teaspoon ground cumin

½ cup coconut milk

Tempering spices

2 tablespoons oil

¼ teaspoon mustard seeds

1 onion, chopped

1 dried red chilli

10 cm (4 in) piece of rampe
(pandanus leaf)

1 small cinnamon stick

5–10 curry leaves (or 1 bay leaf)

Put potatoes, water, salt, fenugreek, garlic, green chilli, tomatoes, turmeric, coriander and cumin in a deep pan and bring to boil over medium heat. Cook until potatoes are firm but soft – about 15 minutes.

In another large pan, heat oil and add mustard seeds. Cook until they pop up – about 30 seconds. Then add other tempering ingredients and heat through until golden brown. Add potato mixture to pan. Stir thoroughly and cook for a further minute until hot right through.

Add coconut milk and bring to boil. Remove from heat and serve with bread, Roti, and rice or Stringhoppers.

Serves 4.

Salted chillies

These chillies add a lot of flavour to vegetarian dishes. Most Sri Lankan kitchens have a jar of salted chillies always at hand, ready to be broken and stirred into curries.

10–15 dried red chillies

500 ml (17 fl oz) water

¼ cup salt

Dissolve the salt in the water and then soak the chillies, for as little as an hour or up to a few days.

Dry cashew curry

This is a wonderful dish that is cooked in Sri Lanka for festive occasions. My mother's eldest sister used to have cashew trees in her garden and we discovered many ways to cook cashews. My mother used to make this dish frequently as it was the simplest way to serve the nuts. She used fresh cashews, which don't need preliminary cooking, but when you buy them in the bag from the supermarket you need to soak them for an hour and then boil them to make them soft again.

2½ cups whole cashews
   (about 385 g/13 oz)
3 cups water for soaking
4 cups water
½ teaspoon turmeric
2 tablespoons oil
2 onions, chopped
½ cinnamon stick
5 cm (2 in) piece of rampe
   (pandanus leaf)

12 curry leaves
¼ teaspoon chilli powder
¼ teaspoon sweet paprika
1 heaped teaspoon Roasted Curry
   Powder (see page 74)
1½ cups coconut milk

Soak cashews in water for about 1 hour. Drain cashews and place in a pan over medium heat with 4 cups fresh water and half the turmeric and boil for 30–35 minutes, until cashews are soft. Drain.

Heat oil in a pan over medium heat, add onion and sauté for 3 minutes. Add cinnamon, rampe and curry leaves and cook for another minute. Add the rest of the turmeric, chilli powder, paprika and roasted curry powder and cook for 30 seconds, taking care not to burn the curry powder.

Add coconut milk and bring to boil. Add cashews and simmer for 5 minutes or until liquid reduces to the level of the cashews. Remove from heat and serve with vegetable curries.

Serves 4.

a vegetarian tradition

The vegetable recipes in this chapter remind me of my mother's vegetarian cravings throughout her life, which, as she later told us, were particularly strong when she was pregnant with my two brothers and me.

When she was pregnant she couldn't eat any meat and was totally dependent on fresh vegetables – this was a spiritual craving, which she said gave her three wonderful sons.

At that time the servants working for us were Gunapala, a 17-year-old boy, and Bailing, a 25-year-old girl. Bailing looked after my mother and Gunapala did the housework and market runs.

As a symbol of motherly love, my grandmother, who lived in a village, would create entire meals for my mother to eat at home in bustling Colombo. Either my grandmother sent servants to Colombo – a one-and-half-hour journey to the city by bus – or my mother would send Gunapala and Bailing to the village to meet my grandmother. Gunapala and Bailing would make the journey early in the morning. They would eat at my grandmother's house and ask her to pray for my mother's health, before taking the food back to Colombo.

Local vendors passed my grandmother's house on their way to market early in the day and would stop to show her their daily offerings. My grandmother would choose the best produce and the vendors were always happy to sell: when the head of the village buys it is viewed as a good omen – it means you will sell everything today. Also, the village's top household won't bargain and won't ask for change from the local vendors.

My grandmother used to announce proudly to the vendors, 'These things are for my town daughter.' It was a great thing to get married and move to the city.

Among the foods on offer were free-range eggs with stunning yellow yolks, which my father loved, and jaggery – solid palm sugar. Most of the fresh fruit and vegetables for sale were grown in what is called a *koratu* – a little section of the backyard every villager had, with space for a pawpaw tree, a jackfruit tree, pumpkin or squash, chilli or tomatoes.

With the day's produce bought, my grandmother and her servants would together cook a huge vegetarian meal, with brown rice from my grandmother's paddies. Dishes included beautiful dry curries, white curries, sambols and mallums. Everything was cooked in clay pots, known as *hatti* and *mutti*, which enhance the spices and make the food smell divine.

My grandmother would then wrap the food, still warm, in banana leaves and local newspaper – everything was wrapped in the news-paper. She made up huge parcels that would feed a whole family – offerings that demonstrated her maternal love. The parcels were packed in a cane basket and the servants would return to my mother before lunchtime. My mother would take her parcels, unwrap them and inhale their aromas. She would eat her meals with my father, and give the extra dishes away.

Cabbage mallum

We in Sri Lanka are not big fans of green salads such as are served in most Western countries; in their place we serve either sambols or a mallum with a meal. Mallums are like a salad, or tabouli, but instead of cracked wheat we use shredded or desiccated coconut. Mallums offset heavy meat curries and rice and provide most of the vitamins in a Sri Lankan diet.

A mallum is made using any green vegetables you have in the garden. The vegetables are thinly shredded and cooked quickly in a little oil and some chilli just until the raw taste is gone. Mallums should be cooked at the last minute and served immediately.

1 tablespoon oil

1 salted chilli (see page 101) – plus an extra 2 for those who like chilli – broken

½ onion, finely sliced

3 cups thinly sliced cabbage

1 cup finely chopped parsley

¼ cup desiccated (shredded) coconut

1 teaspoon salt

¼ teaspoon ground mustard seeds

1 green chilli, sliced

juice of ½ a lime

Heat the oil in a hot pan, add broken salted chillies and cook until they lose their colour – about 2–3 minutes. Add all other ingredients except lime juice and toss over heat for 2 minutes.

Remove from heat. Squeeze lime juice over and serve.

Serves 4 as a side dish.

Variation

You can substitute most vegetables for the cabbage, other than salad leaves: try red cabbage, Asian greens – thinly sliced bok choy, Chinese cabbage – silverbeet or Brussels sprouts.

Beetroot curry

Beetroot curry was the first curry I cooked, at the age of about 17.

2 tablespoons oil

1 onion, chopped

10 cm (4 in) piece of rampe (pandanus leaf) (optional)

10 curry leaves or 2 bay leaves

1 cinnamon stick

2 cloves garlic, sliced

500 g (1 lb 2 oz) beetroot, peeled and sliced or julienned

¼ cup chopped or canned tomatoes

2 green chillies, sliced

1 teaspoon curry powder

¼ teaspoon ground turmeric

¼ teaspoon chilli powder

1 cup water

½ cup coconut milk

salt to taste

Tip

If fresh beetroot is not available, use canned beetroot, but wash it thoroughly to remove the preserving liquid, and cook for just 5 minutes rather than the 7 in the recipe.

Heat the oil in a large pan; add the onion, rampe, curry leaves, cinnamon and garlic and sauté until golden brown – about 1–1½ minutes. Add the beetroot and toss for another 2 minutes.

Add the tomatoes, green chillies, curry powder, turmeric and chilli and stir until spices are mixed through. Add the water, bring to boil then simmer until the beetroot is tender – about 7 minutes. Finally, add the coconut milk and salt to taste.

Serve with a meat dish, or with rice.

Serves 4.

Variation

You can omit the coconut milk and water and stir-fry the rest of the ingredients for a crunchy curry without the sauce. When done like this it is known as a theldala dish. Sri Lankan people like the contrast of one curry with liquid, one pan-fried, at the same meal.

Okra curry

This was one of my mum's favourite dishes and has consequently become one of mine - she loved the fresh flavours in okra and snake bean curries and said okra was good for your brain cells. She always cooked vegetable curries quickly, leaving a crunch in the vegetables.

To most of her curries she also added Maldive fish - dried tuna flakes - for extra flavour. This is optional, and obviously not appropriate for vegetarians.

500 g (1 lb 2 oz) okra, trimmed and cut into 4 cm (1½ in) pieces (instead of okra you can use asparagus or broccoli)

½ teaspoon turmeric

½ teaspoon salt

3 tablespoons oil

10 curry leaves (or 2 bay leaves)

1 teaspoon brown mustard seeds

1 onion, thinly sliced

2 teaspoons dried red chilli flakes

10 cm (4 in) piece of rampe (pandanus leaf) (optional)

1 green chilli

1 teaspoon ground chilli powder

½ teaspoon ground cumin

½ teaspoon ground coriander

1 teaspoon ground turmeric

½ cup chopped or canned tomatoes

salt to taste

1 tablespoon Maldive fish flakes (optional)

½ cup unsweetened coconut milk

1 teaspoon lemon or lime juice

Wash okra and place in a bowl. Toss with turmeric and salt and set aside.

Heat oil in a large pan over medium heat. Add curry leaves, mustard seeds, onion, dried chilli and rampe. Sauté for about 3 minutes but don't let the mustard seeds burn.

Add okra to the pan, then add green chilli, ground chilli powder, cumin, coriander, turmeric and tomato. Cook until lightly brown, tossing all the time so the dry ingredients don't burn. Add salt to taste and Maldive fish flakes for extra flavour.

Add coconut milk, bring to the boil, reduce heat and simmer until okra is cooked — about 7 minutes. Remove from heat, add lemon or lime juice and stir through.

Don't overcook this dish: the okra should still have a light crunch — vegetable curries are always best slightly under-cooked.

Serves 4.

Sweet pumpkin with roasted coconut

¼ cup desiccated (shredded) coconut

½ teaspoon ground mustard seeds

1 small butternut pumpkin (squash), about 680 g (1½ lb) cut into 3 cm (1 1/2 in) cubes

2 cups water

¼–½ cup coconut milk

½ teaspoon salt

Tempering spices

2 tablespoons coconut or vegetable oil

2 salted chillies (see page 101)

1 cinnamon stick

¼ teaspoon fenugreek

¼ teaspoon brown mustard seeds

10 cm (4 in) piece of rampe (pandanus leaf)

10 curry leaves (or 2 bay leaves)

1 onion, chopped

1 clove garlic, crushed

1 cup chopped tomato

Spices

½ teaspoon ground turmeric

1 green chilli, sliced

⅛ teaspoon sweet paprika

1¼ teaspoons salt

⅛ teaspoon chilli powder (optional)

½ teaspoon ground coriander

¼ teaspoon ground cumin

8 peppercorns

Lightly brown coconut and ground mustard seeds in a pan on medium heat – about 30 seconds – taking care not to burn. Set aside. Grind into a paste using a mortar and pestle.

For tempering spices, heat the oil in a large pan over medium heat and add the salted chillies, cinnamon, fenugreek and mustard seeds and cook until mustard seeds pop up – about 20 seconds. Add rampe, curry leaves, onion, garlic and tomato and cook until onion is caramelised – about 2 minutes.

Add pumpkin and spices and sauté for about 1 minute. When well mixed, add water, cover with a lid and cook for about 8–10 minutes, until pumpkin is soft. Add coconut milk and the roasted coconut paste. Mix and cook for a further 2 minutes. Add extra coconut milk if you prefer a thinner liquid. Check flavour; add more salt if desired.

Serve with brown rice or bread.

Serves 4.

Channa's quick vegetable curry

1 cup thick coconut milk

1 cup water

1 cup chicken stock

1 stalk lemongrass, white part only, bruised

10 curry leaves (or 2 bay leaves)

500 g (1 lb 2 oz) pumpkin, peeled and cut into cubes

1 carrot, peeled and cut into cubes the same size as the pumpkin

½ cup cashew nuts

1 tablespoon curry powder

¼ teaspoon saffron or ground turmeric

¼ cup extra coconut milk or water

½ cup frozen peas

1 tablespoon lime juice

salt to taste

½ cup chopped coriander (cilantro) leaves

Place coconut milk, water and chicken stock in a saucepan and bring to the boil. Add the bruised lemongrass and curry leaves and cook for 2 minutes.

Add pumpkin, carrot, nuts, curry powder and saffron and cook until pumpkin is still firm – about 6 minutes. If desired, add extra water or coconut milk for more juice. Add peas and cook for another minute.

Add lime juice and season to taste. Serve with coriander (cilantro) leaves sprinkled on top.

Serves 4.

Variations

- Sometimes I add canned chickpeas instead of frozen peas.

- You can replace the carrot and pumpkin with your favourite vegetables or anything left in the fridge. If adding leafy vegetables such as spinach, bok choy or Asian greens, add them at the last minute, heat through and serve immediately.

- I add ½ teaspoon Maldive fish flakes at the same time as I add the salt, for extra flavour.

Cauliflower, cashew and green pea curry

This is a simple white curry you can make quickly for lunch or dinner. You can add other vegetables, such as carrots and potatoes – whatever is fresh or in the fridge.

1 cup cashews

3 cups water

1 cauliflower, florets only

¼ teaspoon ground turmeric

¼ teaspoon ground cumin

½ teaspoon ground coriander

½ teaspoon salt

½ cup fresh or frozen green peas

½ cup thick coconut milk

2 tablespoons oil

1 onion, chopped

5 curry leaves (or 1 bay leaf)

¼ teaspoon mustard seeds

1 clove garlic, crushed

½ teaspoon dried chilli flakes

1 tablespoon lemon juice

Boil cashews in a large pan in the water until they are tender – for at least 20 minutes – adding more water if necessary.

Add cauliflower, turmeric, cumin, coriander and salt to the cashews and cook for another 5 minutes. Add peas and coconut milk and bring back to the boil.

In another pan heat oil over medium heat, add onion, curry leaves, mustard seeds, garlic and chillies and sauté until golden. Add to the vegetable mixture.

Finish with lemon juice and serve with roti or chunks of plain bread.

Serves 4.

the gift of the gods

Sri Lankans say the coconut palm is a gift of the gods, and every bit of the coconut palm tree plays an important role in their daily lives. Coconuts are a national delicacy in Sri Lanka. Coconut water, especially from the King Coconut, is the perfect drink in the heat of the day, while coconut milk or cream, coconut oil and coconut flesh are used throughout the island's cuisine in everything from curries to sweets. Once the liquids are extracted from coconut flesh, the refuse is used in animal feed.

Coconut has other uses. Coconut leaves are used to make thatched roofs and the trunks are used in constructing houses. Coir, used for mats and ropes, is made of coconut husks and the hard shell is used to make bowls, spoons and ornaments. Even the tree's trunk is used as a giant mortar while the thinner part of the trunk is used as the pestle.

travelling feast

short eats and light snacks

On the streets of Sri Lanka you can smell the snacks around you – the aromas of rotis stuffed with curries, hoppers, savoury doughnuts, pakhoras and deep-fried stuffed banana chillies waft from roadside shops, street vendors' carts, markets and night carnivals.

Short eats are hawker-style food – little bites of flavour eaten on the move – and they are what Sri Lankans love to eat. In bars, beer is served with little tuna cutlets or porkies, which are tiny sausages sautéed with onion, served with a chilli and tomato sauce. At a local cinema, instead of eating popcorn patrons buy potato chips and little savoury snacks, such deep-fried tuna fish and egg balls.

At mid-afternoon, the local baker takes out his tricycle and rides around the villages selling his day's specialties. The trike has two wheels at the front to balance a huge box with a glass front in which he stacks goods sweet and savoury – breads, savoury snacks, rolls with fish or meat fillings, little cakes with butter icing and eclairs dipped in sugar. He rings his bell as he rides and people come from everywhere for an afternoon snack – especially children or women who work in the kitchen.

Food is part of Sri Lanka's street scene all day. Many food shops are open 24 hours and most of the vendors spend all day on the streets, starting at sunrise and ending at night markets feeding people well into the night. Some wheel their carts around different areas and only when everything is quiet on the streets, after 6 or 7 p.m., is their work done.

Uludu wade
savoury urad dhal doughnuts

The word dhal refers to both the dish of lentil purée and the split legumes themselves. Urad dhal is also known as black gram and can be bought from Asian supermarkets and organic shops. You can use green or yellow split peas as an alternative.

2 cups urad dhal
6 cups water
¼ teaspoon bicarbonate of soda
½ teaspoon salt

½ onion, finely chopped
3 green chillies, sliced
10 curry leaves, chopped roughly
oil for deep-frying

Wash the urad dhal and then soak in fresh water overnight, or for at least 6 hours.

After soaking, drain any remaining water; put urad dhal in a food processor and blend to a smooth paste. Add bicarbonate of soda and salt and blend again.

Remove from food processor, place in a bowl with onion, chillies and curry leaves and mix thoroughly.

Rub your palms with oil and, taking a small amount of mixture, roll into the size of a golf ball. Once you have a ball, make a hole right through it with your index finger.

Heat oil in a deep fryer or deep pan, and drop in 4–6 doughnuts at a time, depending on the size of the pan. Cook for 4–5 minutes, until they are golden brown.

Serve with tamarind and coconut chutney or sweet chilli sauce.

Makes 16–18.

Stuffed banana chillies

Banana chillies are a smaller version of capsicums (bell peppers), but they have the long shape of a chilli. You can use small capsicums if you can't find banana chillies.

8 banana chillies or small capsicums (bell peppers)

Filling

2 tablespoons vegetable oil

10 curry leaves

3–4 medium onions, chopped

1 green chilli, deseeded and finely chopped

500 g (1 lb 2 oz) canned, drained tuna or 500 g (1 lb 2 oz) fresh tuna, boiled and flaked

2–3 potatoes, boiled and mashed

¼ teaspoon ground turmeric

10 mint leaves, roughly chopped

salt to taste

pepper to taste

juice of 1 lime

250 g (9 oz) breadcrumbs

oil for deep-frying

Batter

1½ cups plain (all-purpose) flour

½ teaspoon salt

pinch of ground turmeric

½ cup water, or more if necessary

Slit the banana chillies lengthways, but make sure you don't cut into the back or through the ends of the chilli. Use your fingers to remove the seeds. (Don't touch your eyes after this before you have washed your hands thoroughly: you may choose to wear gloves while preparing the chilli.) Then scrape the skin of the chilli with a fork.

Heat the oil in a pan over medium heat, add the curry leaves, onions and green chilli and fry until lightly brown. Add drained tuna, mashed potato, turmeric and mint. Season with salt, pepper and lime juice.

Make a batter: mix all dry ingredients in a bowl. Add water to make a thick batter – you may need to add some extra water.

Put filling into each chilli, making sure it is stuffed into the far end first. It is OK if the chillies expand a bit. Dip each chilli in the batter, roll it in breadcrumbs and deep-fry for 5 minutes or until golden brown.

Place on a tray in an oven preheated to low to keep warm, until all chillies are cooked. Serve with a sweet or hot chilli sauce, and these are great with a beer.

Makes 8.

Beef godambah

Street vendors in Sri Lanka make this short eat. They have bowls of oil holding the little balls of pastry waiting for you to request your favourite filling. This is a tricky recipe but if you take your time you will be well rewarded. You can use beef or chicken for this dish and there are other variations for the filling.

2 potatoes, peeled and cut into quarters

2 tablespoons vegetable oil

1 onion, finely chopped

250 g (9 oz) lean minced (ground) beef or chicken

1 teaspoon crushed dried chilli or chilli flakes

½ cup chopped cabbage

½ cup chopped leek

1 tablespoon lime or lemon juice

½ teaspoon freshly ground black pepper

½ teaspoon salt, or to taste

750 ml (25 fl oz) vegetable oil

Roti dough

2 cups plain (all-purpose) flour

1 cup water

1 teaspoon salt

Boil potatoes for 10 minutes or until soft. Drain off excess water and mash.

Heat the oil in a pan over medium heat. Add the onion and cook until golden brown – about 1 minute. Increase heat to high, add meat and brown it quickly – about 1 minute. Drain any excess liquid.

Add the chilli, cabbage and leek and cook for about 10 minutes, until vegetables are cooked. Drain any excess liquid. Add the potatoes to the pan and mix thoroughly. Add lime or lemon juice and season with pepper and salt, to taste, then set aside.

Continued over page.

Beef godambah

Continued from page 125.

Make roti dough: mix ingredients in a bowl to form a dough and knead for about 3 minutes.

Set aside for 10 minutes to rest then break the dough into 9–10 pieces, each about the size of a golf ball. Roll into balls.

Place vegetable oil in a bowl and place the dough balls in the oil. The balls should sit, covered by the oil. The dough doesn't soak up any oil – the oil simply helps when it comes to thinning the dough out into flat rounds.

Working on a stainless steel top or a pizza tray, take a ball of dough and use your fingers to flatten it out until it is a circle the size of a dinner plate. Take a generous handful of the filling and press into a firm rectangle. Place it at the end of the dough circle closest to you. Fold the sides around the filling so they meet in the centre. Then stretch the short end of pastry closest to you and fold over the filling. Then roll the filling away from you, always thinning out the pastry in front of you and tucking in the corners as you go.

Put a flat non-stick pan over low to medium heat. Place a parcel on the pan and cook for 2–3 minutes. Turn over to cook all four long sides, then stand upright and cook both ends. While you are doing this, continue making more cubes and add them to the pan as you go.

Serve with a sweet or hot chilli sauce.

Makes 9–10.

Filling variations

● Instead of leek and cabbage, fillings can be made of peas and corn, spinach and pumpkin, carrots or sweet potatoes.

● Chop vegetables into cubes and boil but do not overcook.

● The mashed potato is essential to hold the mixture together; you can, however, substitute mashed pumpkin for it.

● You can also add ½ cup chopped coriander (cilantro) at the end for a beautiful flavour.

Ala bonda

2 tablespoons yellow split peas

1 cup water

3 potatoes, peeled and cut into 1 cm (½ in) cubes

4 cups water, or enough to cover potatoes

1 teaspoon salt

4 tablespoons oil

1 teaspoon mustard seeds

6 curry leaves

1 onion, finely chopped

1 teaspoon crushed ginger

1 teaspoon crushed garlic

1 green chilli, chopped

½ teaspoon salt

½ teaspoon ground turmeric

oil for deep-frying

Batter

100 g (3½ oz) chickpea flour (besan flour)

50 g (2 oz) rice flour

¼ teaspoon sweet paprika

¼ teaspoon ground turmeric

½ teaspoon salt

¾ cup water, or more if necessary

Soak lentils for 4 hours. Drain and place lentils in a pot with 1 cup water and boil for 5 minutes. Drain and set aside.

In a pot over medium heat put potatoes, water and salt to cover, and boil until the potatoes are just cooked — only about 5 minutes as the potatoes need to be firm. Drain and set aside.

Heat oil in a pan over medium heat. Add the mustard seeds and cook for 10 seconds, until they pop up. Add the curry leaves and lentils and cook until lightly browned — about 30 seconds. Add onion, ginger, garlic, green chilli, salt and turmeric. Stir through and cook for 30 seconds. Add potatoes, stir through and remove from heat.

Make a batter: place all dry ingredients in a bowl and mix. Make a well in the centre and add enough water to make a thick, dripping batter.

Take enough of the potato filling to make a mound slightly bigger than a golf ball. Dip it in the batter (you might like to use a fork to dip the ball into the batter and then remove it). Let the ball drip, but don't shake off any 'excess' batter. Once it has just stopped dripping, drop in hot oil and deep-fry for 5 minutes, or until golden brown. Once fried, place on a plate in a hot oven until the whole batch is cooked.

Serve warm with a sweet chilli dipping sauce or a sambol.

Serves 6–8.

Tuna fish balls

2 tablespoons vegetable oil

10 curry leaves

3–4 onions, chopped

1 green chilli, deseeded and finely
   chopped

500 g (1 lb 2 oz) canned, drained
   tuna or 500 g (1 lb 2 oz) fresh
   tuna, boiled and flaked

2–3 potatoes, boiled and mashed

¼ teaspoon ground turmeric

10 mint leaves, roughly chopped

salt to taste

pepper to taste

juice of 1 lime

breadcrumbs

oil for deep-frying

Batter

1½ cups plain (all-purpose) flour

½ teaspoon salt

½ cup water

Heat the 2 tablespoons oil in a pan over medium heat, add the curry leaves, onions and green chilli and fry until lightly brown. Add drained tuna and heat through for 2 minutes. Add mashed potato, turmeric and mint. Mix well and season with salt, pepper and lime juice.

Make batter: put flour and salt in a bowl and mix well. Make a well in the centre and add enough water to make a thick dripping batter.

Shape tuna mixture into small balls or croquettes. Dip in batter, coat in breadcrumbs and deep-fry until golden brown. Serve with tomato or sweet chilli sauce.

Makes 20.

Tips

● Adding mint is something my mum used to do. Most people use just curry leaves.

● Add more green chilli or pepper for extra spice.

the little monk

This young Buddhist monk is standing behind a senior monk's robe, a robe the young boy has washed and hung out to dry. Part of a young monk's life consists of voluntarily helping the monk elders – that's how they learn about good karma. Helping others in this life will assist them in enlightenment.

Some young boys start their training as monks at eight years of age but others can be teenagers, in their twenties or even older, before they choose the religious life. Sometimes when children are born, their horoscopes reveal they have a bad future waiting for them. Then the only thing the family can do is give the boy to the temple to rid the child of its bad karma. Sri Lankans are strong believers in fate.

But most young monks are boys who simply see the older monks and decide that this is the life they want to lead. We believe they were monks in a past life and they choose to become monks again to continue the life circle.

If a young boy asks to become a monk, the villagers hold a huge ceremony. The young man is dressed in finery fit for a king and paraded on the street, with his parents behind him and relatives and friends at his side. This is a test – if the boy likes the feeling of material wealth and having people's attention, then he cannot be a monk. It takes great courage for a little boy not to be swayed by the material possessions and the crowd.

Once he makes his decision he either goes back to life with his family or he shaves his head and goes to live at the monastery to begin his life as a monk. Here he is taught about Buddhism in depth as well as normal studies, which can lead to university.

Buddhist monks eat sparsely. They eat breakfast early in the morning and then usually have a vegetarian meal before noon. Buddhist monks only eat dinner if they are unwell.

At one stage, after my father had died, I went a temple for about two months to live as an *upasaka*, a person taking a course of 10 disciplines, which is more than the five disciplines every person should take each day. I wore white robes and meditated. I wanted to know what life was all about, and to find peace at a trying time.

It was an extremely difficult life, but one day I announced that I didn't want to leave. The head monk said that even though I was well disciplined as an *upasaka* I had unfinished work and I had to go home. My experience is typical: you become attached to the ashram as a way of counselling, as a place to become grounded when emotions sweep you away.

Many Sri Lankans talk to monks when they have trouble in their lives. They ask: 'What am I going to do?' The monk will explain the solution in calm manner: 'Think about it in a Buddhist way,' he will say. Even though there has often been civil war in Sri Lanka, we are a peace-loving people.

"If a young boy asks to become a monk, the villagers hold a huge ceremony. The young man is dressed in finery fit for a king and paraded on the street, with his parents behind him and relatives and friends at his side. This is a test – if the boy likes the feeling of material wealth and having people's attention, then he cannot be a monk. It takes great courage for a little boy not to be swayed by the material possessions and the crowd."

Parrippu wade

1 cup split peas

water for soaking

extra ¼ cup water

1 onion, finely chopped

½ teaspoon mustard seeds

1 green chilli, chopped

1 clove garlic, chopped

½ teaspoon dried red chilli flakes

2 teaspoons chickpea flour
   (besan flour)

½ teaspoon salt

vegetable oil for deep-frying

Wash and drain split peas. Place peas in a dish with enough water to cover and soak overnight, or for at least 6 hours.

Drain split peas and place in a food processor with the ¼ cup water. Add all remaining ingredients except oil for frying. Pulse blend until mixture is combined but still rough. Remove and place in a bowl.

Rub your palms with oil, take a small amount of mixture – about the size of a golf ball – roll it into a ball then press down into a patty about 1 cm (½ in) thick. Set aside and continue to make patties with the rest of the mixture. You may place them in the fridge before cooking.

Deep-fry in batches for 4–5 minutes, or until golden brown.

Makes 16–18.

Lamb patties

2 potatoes, peeled and cut into quarters

2 tablespoons vegetable oil

1 onion, finely chopped

250 g (9 oz) minced (ground) lamb

1 teaspoon crushed dried chilli or chilli flakes

½ teaspoon freshly ground black pepper

¼ teaspoon ground turmeric

½ teaspoon salt

½ cup chopped cabbage

½ cup chopped leek

1 tablespoon lime or lemon juice

Pastry

2 cups plain (all-purpose) flour

½ teaspoon salt

⅓ cup butter or ghee

½ cup iced water

½ teaspoon cumin seeds

yolk of 1 egg

Boil potatoes for 10 minutes or until soft. Drain off excess water and mash. Set aside.

Heat the oil in a pan over medium heat. Add the onion and cook until golden brown – about 1 minute. Increase heat to high, add meat and brown it quickly – about 1 minute. Drain any excess liquid. Add the rest of the ingredients except the lime juice and cook for about 10 minutes, until leek and cabbage are cooked. Drain any excess liquid.

Add the potatoes to the pan and mix thoroughly. Add lime or lemon juice and check for salt to taste. Set aside.

Make pastry: rub flour, salt and butter together. Add water gradually until mixture forms a dough. Add cumin and knead for 3 minutes. Cover with plastic wrap and place in the fridge for 15–20 minutes to rest.

Roll dough out until about 2 mm (⅛ in) thick. Cut into circles slightly smaller than a saucer. Place a small ball of lamb filling in the middle, brush one end with egg yolk and fold pastry over. Press edge with a fork to seal.

Cover a tray with cooking paper. Dust with flour. Arrange patties on the tray without touching each other. Leave in the fridge for at least 20 minutes. Deep-fry in batches for 5 minutes until golden brown.

Makes 8–10.

Tip

You can make smaller patties if you are eating them as finger food.

Pakhoras

Sri Lankan culture has its origins in Indian culture and as a result the food exhibits a strong Indian influence. Pakhoras in particular have their origin in Indian cuisine, but this is how we make them in Sri Lanka.

2 cups chickpea flour
  (besan flour)
1 teaspoon crushed ginger
1 green chilli, chopped
½ teaspoon chilli powder
¼ teaspoon ground turmeric
¼ teaspoon bicarbonate of soda
1½ teaspoons salt, or to taste

½ cup water
½ cup natural yoghurt
1 tablespoon lemon juice
1 cup thinly sliced onion
1 cup thinly sliced carrots
½ cup roughly chopped coriander
  (cilantro) leaves
oil for deep-frying

Put the flour, ginger, green chilli, chilli powder, turmeric, bicarbonate of soda, salt, water, yoghurt and lemon juice into a bowl. Combine to form a thick dough, adding extra flour if needed. (This dough mixture can be kept in the fridge for about a week.)

When ready to cook, mix the vegetables and coriander in a bowl, add the dough and mix thoroughly. There should be just enough dough to hold the vegetables together roughly.

Take small handfuls of the mixture and make irregular balls, roughly the size of a golf ball. Place on a tray and leave to rest in the fridge for about 10 minutes.

Heat oil for deep-frying, and drop in 4–6 at a time, depending on the size of the pot. Cook for 4–5 minutes, or until golden brown and crispy.

Serve warm with mango chutney or a sweet chutney.

Makes 15–16.

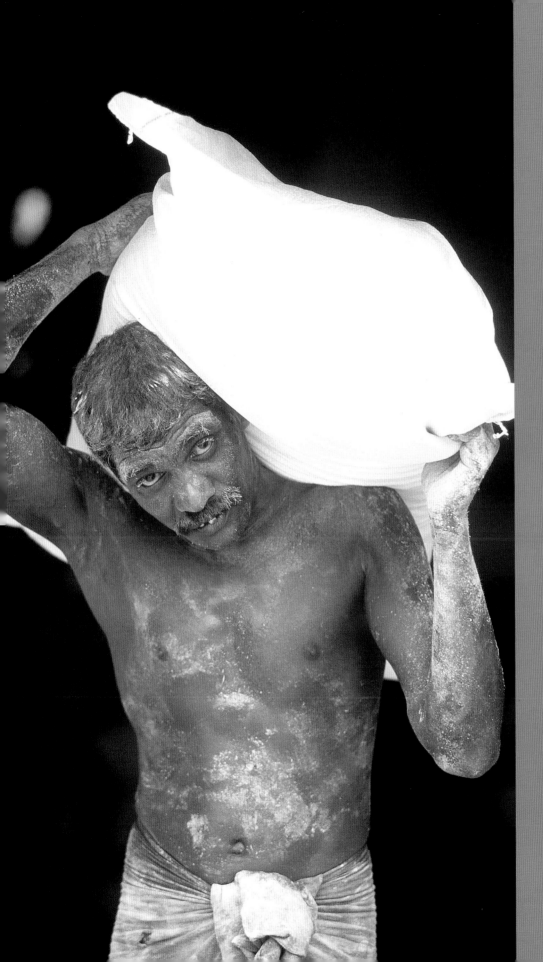

Bags of wheat flour are carried from a lorry to a storeroom by workers who are paid by the day or by the job. It is hard work and at the end of the day they look like ghosts, covered in flour.

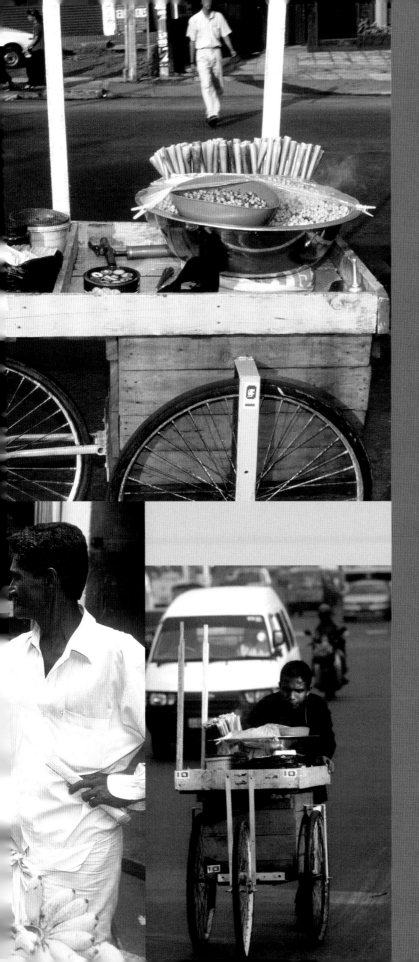

hawker food

Many Sri Lankan food vendors carry out their business using three-wheeled carts, selling their goods from a tray on the top. Most of the carts have a tiny kerosene burner, which is used for cooking and as a light at night.

Small rotis stuffed with meat or vegetables, or small lentil wades (doughnuts) are deep-fried and served hot, while chickpeas are tossed over a hot flame with chilli and salt and served in cones of newspaper as a snack. The carts usually have a bell which tells people the cart man is on his way.

sweet
treats

sweet meats
and drinks

Sri Lankan cuisine is not known for its desserts, and a traditional Sri Lankan family dinner does not follow the same pattern as a Western meal, which usually ends with a pudding or sweet dessert of some sort.

Sweet meats, as the little Sri Lankan desserts are called, are in fact sometimes served before the meal. For instance, little oil cakes may be presented to dinner guests with a cup of tea before the main meal. That said, traditions change and these days in Sri Lanka you may be served a small piece of wattalappan or bread and butter pudding following the main meal.

Sweet meats are more commonly enjoyed for morning or afternoon tea, when you then might eat pol pani pancakes and delicious love cakes. And at almost any time of the day, Sri Lankans eat curd, which is produced from the roaming buffalo herds, and sold in little clay pots drizzled with treacle.

While Sri Lankans may not be big dessert eaters, drinking tea is a national pastime. Tea is one of Sri Lanka's two main export crops, the other being coconut products. Most of the tea is grown in the hill country with its warm climate, perfect altitude and sloping terrain.

Tea is served in many forms, either as simple black leaf tea with milk and jaggary - palm sugar - or spiced with herbs, cinnamon, ginger or lemon. Tea is constantly available in every home and sold by roadside cafés and street vendors. It is rare to have a social gathering without it.

Pol pani pancakes

This is one of my favourite sweets. My mother used to make pol pani pancakes for afternoon tea. We would come home from school, have lunch and snooze. Then we would wake up about 4 p.m. and mum would produce pol pani pancakes and warm tea. I use a ladle to make pancakes so I always know how much batter I am pouring into the pan. If you don't have a ladle, put the mixture into a jug and then pour enough for a pancake into the pan.

1 egg

2½ cups milk or unsweetened coconut milk

135 g (4½ oz) plain (all-purpose) flour

pinch of salt

pinch of ground turmeric

2 tablespoons melted butter

Lightly beat egg and milk together in a bowl.

Put flour and dry ingredients in another bowl, make a well and pour milk and egg into it. Mix to make a batter. Add melted butter and mix well. Cover with plastic wrap and leave in the fridge for about 20 minutes.

Stir well before using. If the batter is too thick, add a little milk and stir through.

Grease a small pan, then warm pan on medium heat. Stir batter and pour about 3–4 tablespoons of batter into the pan. Swirl pan around so pancake covers the base of the pan, making a circle about the size of a saucer. Cook for 30 seconds–1 minute, depending on how thick the batter is.

Flip with a spatula, cook the other side until it is brown and remove from pan. Dust pancakes with sugar as you stack them so they don't stick. Serve with filling, see pol pani filling recipe on this page.

Makes about 14 pancakes.

Pol pani filling

This filling will keep in the fridge for weeks and can be used when you make a fresh batch of pancakes. It can also be served after a main meal, with a scoop of vanilla ice cream.

250 g (9 oz) jaggery (palm sugar) or brown sugar

2 cups water

3 cardamom pods, crushed

3 cloves

½ teaspoon ground pepper

15 cm (6 in) piece of rampe (pandanus leaf), cut into 3–4 pieces

2½ cups desiccated (shredded) coconut

½ teaspoon lemon juice

Chop or grate jaggery into a bowl. Add water, cardamom, cloves, pepper and rampe, bring to boil and continue to boil for 5 minutes. Add coconut and stir over low heat for 3–4 minutes.

Remove from heat and add lemon juice. Remove rampe.

Take one pancake, place 2 tablespoons filling across one end and roll pancake up.

Wattalappan

Wattalappan is a Sri Lankan version of cream caramel, but palm sugar is used instead of white sugar and coconut milk instead of cow's milk. The spices add a particular Sri Lankan flavour. Cashews are expensive in Sri Lanka so garnishing curries, desserts, sweet meats and rices with a topping of nuts is usually only done for special occasions and festive meals.

650 ml (22 fl oz) coconut milk

275 g (10 oz) palm sugar, grated or brown sugar

6 eggs

2 egg yolks

good pinch each of ground cinnamon, cloves, nutmeg and cardamom

50 g (2 oz) cashews, roughly chopped

Preheat oven to 160°C (320°F).

Place coconut milk and sugar in a pan and stir over low heat until the sugar has dissolved. Set aside to cool.

Lightly beat eggs and yolks together in a bowl and strain coconut milk over the eggs. Strain again. Add spices and mix well. Pour into a 20 cm (8 in) diameter ovenproof glass dish or individual dishes. Sprinkle cashews on top and cover with greaseproof paper. Place dish in a pan of water and bake in the oven for 40–45 minutes.

The dish is cooked when the surface bounces back when touched and a skewer comes out clean.

Serves 4–6.

Tip

Palm sugar is found under several names: you may see it being sold as gulab melaka or jaggery.

Bread and butter pudding

My mother always used leftover bread from the previous day for this recipe. I learnt to cook a variation of this traditional dish when I was working at the Hilton and used to make it for my mother. Fresh bread is fine for this recipe, but bread and butter pudding is all about using leftover ingredients. If you have any, use leftover croissants, sliced roughly into 1 cm (½ in) pieces, for a deliciously buttery pudding, or leftover cake.

1½ cups sugar

1 tablespoon water

50 g (2 oz) sugar

4 large eggs

1 teaspoon vanilla essence or
  2 tablespoons rum or Baileys
  Irish Cream

300 ml (10 fl oz) milk

300 ml (10 fl oz) double cream

½ loaf of sliced bread – about
  200 g (7 oz)

80 g (3 oz) softened butter

50 g (2 oz) sultanas or frozen
  blueberries

sugar for sprinkling

Preheat the oven to 180°C (350°F).

Place sugar and water in a pot over medium heat. Leave in the pan for 5–6 minutes until mixture has turned into a golden brown caramel. Take care not to burn or over-colour it – the sugar will taste burnt if you leave it colouring for too long.

Pour the caramel into a 25 cm (12 in) square ovenproof dish, to cover the bottom of the pan. Set aside.

Cream the sugar and eggs together. Add vanilla or alcohol, mix well. Add milk and cream and stir through.

Arrange half the bread in overlapping pieces in the dish on top of the caramel. Dab with a few pieces of soft butter. Add sultanas or blueberries. Arrange the rest of the bread in the dish. Pour the custard over the bread and push the bread down into the custard to soak. Sprinkle the top with sugar.

Place a deep tray filled with water on the bottom shelf in the oven. Place the pudding in the oven and cook for 40–50 minutes. Remove and let stand for a few minutes before serving. Serve with ice cream or your favourite jam.

Serves 6–8.

Variations

- You can make this dish with bananas instead of sultanas or blueberries.

- For a richer mixture, use 2 large eggs and 2 egg yolks instead of 4 eggs.

In many rural areas of Sri Lanka there are no water pipelines; instead the villages have tube wells from which they can pump water. It is often the task of young girls to walk to the wells, which can be up to a couple of kilometres from the village, to fetch the daily water supply in an aluminium pot.

Love cake

My mentor Dur-é Dara has contributed the following two recipes. Dur-é writes:
My grandmother grew up in Sri Lanka but travelled to Malaysia as a young woman. There she met a man from the Sri Lankan city of Jaffna and they eventually married and had six children, my mother among them.

Although my grandparents lived in Malaysia they maintained many of their Sri Lankan food customs and habits and I grew up every Christmas partaking in the family activity of dicing vast quantities of fruit and mixing cakes in big baby baths. Sri Lankans traditionally eat these semolina cakes at Christmas. They are similar to standard fruit cakes but slightly richer and stickier. I have since seen the cakes on the menus of several restaurants in Melbourne. My 80-year-old aunt still makes these Christmas and Love cakes and sends them to relatives and friends in America, England and Australia.

250 g (9 oz) semolina
125 g (4 oz) butter
10 eggs
500 g (1 lb 2 oz) castor (superfine) sugar
185 g (6 oz) cashew nuts, chopped finely
2 tablespoons rosewater

2 tablespoons honey
¼ teaspoon grated nutmeg
¼ teaspoon lemon rind
½ teaspoon ground cardamom
¼ teaspoon ground cinnamon

Preheat oven to 150°C (300°F). Place semolina on an oven tray and place in the oven for 5 minutes to warm through. Soften butter and mix with warm semolina.

Separate eggs, set whites aside.

Beat egg yolks and castor sugar together until light and creamy. Add semolina and butter and beat until well mixed. Add nuts, rosewater, honey, nutmeg, lemon rind, cardamom and cinnamon and mix together.

Beat egg whites until they form peaks. Fold whites into cake mixture. Pour into a lined shallow slice tin and bake in the oven for an hour. The cake is cooked when an inserted skewer comes out clean.

Serve in slices.

Christmas cake

This is a moist, soft cake, like a heavy plum pudding, often used for Sri Lankan wedding cakes.

250 g (9 oz) preserved ginger

250 g (9 oz) glacé cherries

250 g (9 oz) cashews

250 g (9 oz) mixed glacé fruit

250 g (9 oz) raisins

375 g (13 oz) sultanas

125 g (4 oz) mixed peel

500 g (1 lb 2 oz) ginger jam

½ cup brandy

375 g (13 oz) butter

500 g (1 lb 2 oz) castor
(superfine) sugar

12 egg yolks

1 tablespoon honey

1½ teaspoons ground cardamom

1 teaspoon ground cinnamon

1 teaspoon grated nutmeg

¾ teaspoon ground cloves

2 teaspoons grated lemon rind

1 tablespoon vanilla essence

1 tablespoon almond essence

2 teaspoons rose essence

250 g (9 oz) semolina

6 egg whites

extra brandy

Almond icing

250 g (9 oz) ground almonds

500 g (1 lb 2 oz) icing
(confectioner's) sugar

1 small egg, beaten

1 tablespoon brandy

1 tablespoon sherry

½ teaspoon almond essence

½ teaspoon beaten egg white

Preheat oven to 140°C (275°F). Prepare a 25 cm (10 in) round or square tin with three thickness of brown paper and two layers of greaseproof paper brushed with melted butter.

Drain syrup from preserved ginger and chop ginger into small pieces. Cut cherries into quarters, cut nuts finely or grind them.

Combine all fruit and nuts in a large bowl with the ginger jam and brandy and leave to soak for 4 hours or overnight.

Cream butter and sugar together until light. Add egg yolks one at a time, beating well. Add honey, spices, grated rind and essences and mix well. Add semolina and continue to beat. Add fruit mixture and stir well using your hands. Finally, whip egg whites until stiff and fold through.

Place mixture in prepared cake tin and bake for 2–2½ hours; cover the cake with greaseproof paper for the first 1¼ hours in the oven.

Stand to cool. When cool sprinkle brandy over cake before icing, preferably the following day (wrap in foil overnight).

To make icing, put ground almonds, icing sugar, egg, brandy, sherry and almond essence in a bowl and stir with a spoon to form a thick paste. Ice cake and then brush beaten egg white over it.

Place cake in airtight container – it will keep for a year or longer.

sacred creatures

When we were small children my parents used to take us for a week or two once a year, in the August school holidays, into the jungle of the Yala National Wildlife Park on Sri Lanka's south-east coast to relax, leaving behind politics and business.

My parents would pack our bags and we would travel to a bungalow in the middle of the jungle. Once there we wouldn't be able to leave until the week was up and so we would have to carry in all our food. We would not be alone: there was always a tracker staying with us, a caretaker for the bungalow and people to cook the meals. The bungalow didn't have electricity but ran on kerosene, and we would have barbecues each day.

In front of the bungalow was an amazing tree which we could climb up and sit in. From the treetop there were wonderful views of the lake below. At night we would take our food and drink, climb into the tree and watch the elephants in the moonlight drinking from the lake. There were no radios, just the jungle and the voice of the birds and wildlife.

Elephants are held in high regard in Sri Lanka and it was once seen as a hideous crime to kill an elephant. Historically, it was a sign of wealth to own an elephant, but these days they are endangered species and the exorbitant cost of owning an elephant means they are rarely a family pet .

Those who have a domestic elephant – there are about 300 in the country – employ a *mahout*, or elephant keeper, and it is his full-time job to feed and bathe the mammoth creature. Elephants are sometimes seen strolling along the roadside in rural Sri Lanka with the mahute behind, walking to a place to bathe or to take part in a festival.

In the past, elephants were used to cart timber and other heavy loads, but it is not a common practice now. An elephant orphanage near Kegalle is run by the government and looks after abandoned or orphaned elephants.

Sri Lanka has many elaborate and colourful festivals throughout the year. One of the most important is the *Asala Perahera* (meaning parade or procession). This 10-day event is held in July–August and honours the Sacred Tooth of the Buddha, which is enshrined in the *Dalada Maligawa* (the Temple of the Tooth), in Kandy. The procession involves thousands of Kandyan dancers and drummers and a parade of more than 50 elephants covered in brilliant cloaks.

Curd and treacle

Curd and treacle is one of Sri Lanka's most popular desserts and is often sold on the beaches of the south coast by street vendors for about 50 cents a pot. It is also served on special occasions such as a wedding buffet, religious feast or festival.

Traditionally in Sri Lanka the curd is made from the milk of the herds of buffalos that roam along the roadsides. It is then allowed to set in a clay pot known as a kiri hatti, which is also made by villagers.

Once the curd has been eaten people use the pots for cooking, or add wire and fill them with hanging plants.

Others put a hole in the bottom, paint the pot with white dots and nail it to the wall at the front of the house to attract sparrows to nest.

Greek-style set yoghurt is similar to the buffalo curd we eat in Sri Lanka. It's good for the digestion, containing health-promoting bacteria.

It is best served with jaggery – solid palm sugar – cane sugar or treacle. You can even use golden syrup if you can't find any of the others.

1 cup yoghurt
2 tablespoons treacle

Take the yoghurt out of the pot, place it in a bowl and pour the treacle over the top. I love the sugary taste, so tend to add 3 table-spoons of treacle, but it is up to the individual.

Serves 1.

travelling salesmen

A man carrying pots over his shoulders - a common way of transporting things in rural Sri Lanka - wanders into the village and shouts, 'I've got flower pots, I've got normal pots.' A woman cooking in her kitchen remembers she needs pots and runs out to the street. She claps her hands to draw the vendor's attention to buy a pot.

Clay pots are the most common cooking vessel in a Sri Lankan kitchen. The pots are blackened by the fire but give dishes a wonderfully distinct flavour.

It is tradition to buy a new pot before each New Year's Day. When the new year begins you boil the milk in the new pot letting it spill over the sides. This is said to bring prosperity for the coming year.

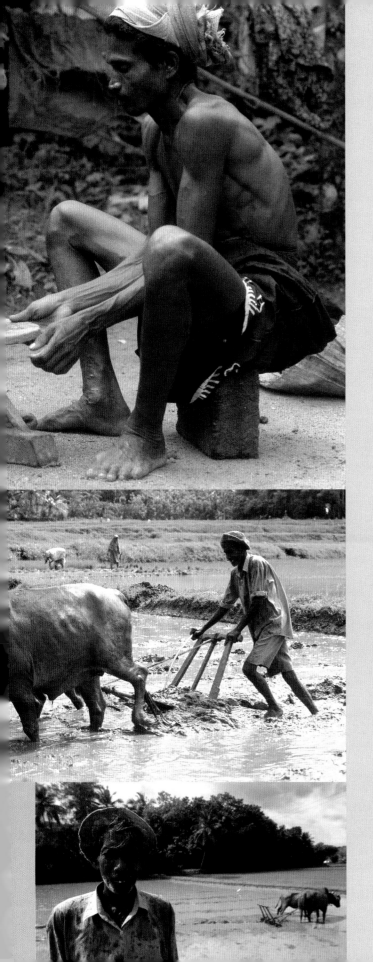

essential tasks

In my grandmother's village, all essential tasks are divided up between the local people so, as a village, the community can support itself. Some people farm and some make clay bricks for houses, while others make clay pots or grow vegetables. As a community they have people locally producing what is needed, so they don't have to travel to faraway places to buy essential items.

Trades are passed from father to son or mother to daughter or the entire family works on a particular task. If you want to buy bricks there is a certain section in the village where everyone makes bricks, while pots will be made in another area, and so on.

These days, the current generation of children goes to school, so the traditional trades are in danger of being lost. When children are educated they look for less traditional jobs and professions such as doctors and lawyers, and they want different lives to their parents.

But it is good to see these tasks still being performed locally. Here, an old lady teaches a young man the tradition of pot making. The pots are used for cooking or for flowers, or to keep water in, as most of the villagers don't have running water in their houses.

tea

Tea is one of Sri Lanka's main export crops and drinking it is a national pastime. Tea is served at all times of the day, either black, with milk or milk powder when fresh milk is not available and with sugar, jaggery or spices such as ginger. Tea is always served to visitors when they arrive at a Sri Lankan home and can be bought from roadside stalls in most streets throughout the country.

Spiced tea

4 cups water

3 cardamom pods

1 cinnamon stick

1 slice of ginger

2 cloves

4 heaped teaspoons black tea leaves

4 teaspoons condensed milk

Place water and spices in a pot and bring to the boil over medium heat. Remove from the heat, add tea and leave for 2–3 minutes. Serve with condensed milk on the side and add to taste.

Serves 4.

Variation

Instead of serving with condensed milk, add ½ cup milk to the water when you add the tea and serve with 2 tablespoons honey on the side.

Cinnamon tea

4 cups water

1 cinnamon stick

4 teaspoons sugar

4 heaped teaspoons black tea leaves

½ cup milk

Place water, cinnamon and sugar in a pot and bring to the boil. Remove from heat and add tea. Stand to draw for 3–4 minutes. Add milk to the pot, stir and serve with sugar if necessary.

Serves 4.

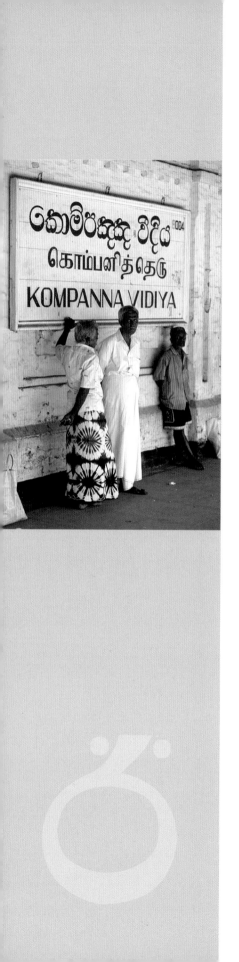

tea

Ginger tea

4 cups water
5 slices of ginger
4 teaspoons black tea leaves
½ cup milk

Place water and ginger in a pot and bring to boil. Add tea and stand to rest for 2–3 minutes. Add milk, stir through and serve with sugar if needed.

Serves 4.

Lemon tea

4 cups water
4 teaspoons heaped black tea leaves
lime or lemon cut into wedges

Place water in a pot and bring to boil. Remove from heat. Add tea. Stand to draw for 2–3 minutes. Serve in a teapot with a wedge of lime or lemon on the side waiting to be squeezed in.

Serves 4.

Faluda

This dish shows the Muslim influence in Sri Lankan sweets and drinks. You can buy basil seeds in Asian grocery shops, but you can also make this drink without them.

1 teaspoon basil seeds (optional)
½ cup water
1 tablespoon rose syrup
2 cups milk
1 scoop vanilla ice cream

Soak basil seeds in water until needed. When ready to make drink, drain seeds.

In a tall glass mix the rose essence, milk and basil seeds. Stir well, add ice cream and serve with a long spoon and a big straw.

Serves 1.

Variation

In Sri Lanka people make a green jelly, cut it into 5 mm (¼ in) cubes and add a tablespoon of green jelly cubes to the drink.

Mango lassi

Lassis are part of the Indian influence on Sri Lankan cuisine. My mother used to add three or four pieces of fresh mango to a lassi. She would make us lassis in the morning before we went to school, or when fresh mangoes or bananas were in abundance. Like most Sri Lankans, mum used buffalo curd instead of yoghurt.

3 tablespoons mango purée
2 tablespoons plain yoghurt
1 cup milk

Blend ingredients and serve in a tall glass.

Serves 1.

Variations

● To make a sweet lassi, replace the mango with 1 tablespoon sugar. For a savoury lassi use a pinch of salt.

● Low-fat milk and yoghurt can be used as an alternative to full-cream varieties.

● You can substitute strawberries or raspberries for mango.

opening the doors on traditional Sri Lanka

High in Sri Lanka's Hill Country, amid the traditional villages, sits one of the world's most environmentally friendly hotels. Long and low, the Kandalama Hotel winds dramatically around a rocky outcrop on the edge of an ancient tank (an artificial lake built for irrigation). The hotel is hidden in the Hill Country, 170 km north-east of Colombo and 85 km north of Kandy, surrounded by lakes and forests inhabited by spectacular wildlife, trees more than a century old, rare plants and birds. The area also is home to two UNESCO world heritage sites – the Dambulla rock temple which dates from the first century b.c. and the fifth century a.d. Sigiriya rock fortress.

The Kandalama Hotel is one of the world's finest examples of sustainable tourism development. Designed by Sri Lanka's most prolific and famous architect, Geoffrey Bawa, the hotel was created to have as little affect on the local environment as possible. It is run in an ecologically sustainable manner - water is recycled for irrigation and sewage is turned into compost.

Born in 1919, Geoffrey Bawa is best known for his ability to incorporate the climate, landscape and culture of ancient Ceylon into his architecture. Among the most famous of his buildings are the Bentota Beach Hotel (1968), Sri Lanka's 1979 Parliament House and Ruhunu University near Matara.

Index